GOOD

The Study Society and the editors are grateful
to Mr Jaiswal, Mr Agrawal, and Mr Dixit
who acted as verbatim interpreters at the
audiences with His Holiness.

Thanks are also due to the
School of Meditation, London,
for some excerpts.

Helen O' Sullivan

GOOD COMPANY

An Anthology of sayings, stories
and answers to questions by

His Holiness
Sri Shantanand Saraswati
The Shankaracharya of
Jyotir Math, Northern India

© Vega 2002
Text © The Study Society 1987, 1992, 2002

ISBN 1-84333-047-4

A catalogue record for this book is available
from the British Library

First published by the Study Society, London, 1987
and in 2002 by
Vega
64 Brewery Road
London, N7 9NT

A member of Chrysalis Books plc

Visit our website at www.chrysalisbooks.co.uk

Printed in Great Britain
by CPD, Wales

Contents

Introduction

This book is for refreshment, for clarity of mind and heart, and for the private recollection of important ideas by people practising the meditation which is mentioned throughout.

The book is arranged so that it may be read in several different ways: it may be read consecutively, following the sequences of themes set out in the table of contents; or it may be read, using the table of contents and the index, to follow up a particular idea or for the purpose of finding extracts that have relevance to circumstances in the reader's life. It may also be read by using the running headings at the top of each page to find whatever seems right for the time or place.

It does not matter which way the book is used, since every part of the discourses is essentially all of a piece with H.H.'s teaching as a whole, based on direct knowledge of the unity underlying life in all its manifestations.

H.H.'s discourses include many Sanskrit words. Whenever possible, these have been translated into English, but in some cases there is no equivalent in English. The meaning of these words will grow deeper as the reader assimilates the contents of the anthology as a whole.

The term 'Atman' signifies the individual Self and the term 'Param-Atman' means the Universal Self, of which the Atman is an atom of the same substance, with all the same properties.

'Param-Atman is the Atman of the whole Universe, living and non-living, conceivable and inconceivable.'

1 Unity of Creation

Within and without are the same. The Absolute is in all. All beings are a part of the same. Everything exists in Atman and it is also reflected in the human form. Wherever you look, you look at the Atman. It is not so much a question of looking within or without, but a question of looking rightly or wrongly.

The Absolute is Truth, Consciousness and Bliss. The creation is for bliss. It is a play, and the play is only for enjoyment. Human beings are also the Absolute and include everything the Absolute has. Men are self-truthful, self-consciousful and self-blissful. The Absolute creates and enjoys without getting involved, only as a witness, but man prefers to enjoy as a doer and not as a witness. This claim is followed by the duality of 'want it' and 'got it'. All this binds man in little boundaries and little boundaries give him only little bliss. The Self, being the Absolute, could not be satisfied with such little bliss, and this is why there is a constant search for more bliss, more truth and more consciousness. The search makes men overactive and run amok which is followed by troubles, anxieties, conflicts and discomfort. The real purpose is thus completely lost. Only if men could see that they have nothing to do, nothing to claim, nothing to achieve in this already complete and blissful creation, they would begin to enjoy and also fulfil the purpose.

Somehow we have forgotten that the Absolute is immanent everywhere and is ready to meet us with its full force. It is not only in Samadhi that one meets the Absolute with full force; the Absolute is ready to meet you as a table, as a chair, as food, and in everything. It is ignorance which has covered our vision; we have to come out of this ignorance and we cannot do it unless we go into meditation. When we have learnt to come very close to this undifferentiated unity of the Self, then we will see that the Absolute, which appears to be outside and seemingly separated, becomes united with us. Then there is no beginning, there is no end, there is no inner and there is no outer—it is the same Absolute available everywhere and there is never any separation.

Whenever any unity is experienced it immediately brings bliss into actions, and this can only happen when consciousness is active. All unity takes place in consciousness and in every conscious act there is this bliss supporting itself. When one takes food, perhaps a piece of fruit, and one tastes and experiences the freshness of the juice, a little bliss bursts out in the enjoyment of eating and the sweetness of the taste. The Vedas declare the Absolute as 'Rasa Vai Sah', 'He is the juice or essence'. This bursting out of the enjoyment, even in eating an ordinary thing like fruit, is in essence an experience of the consciousness of the Absolute himself, because the Absolute has manifested himself as the juice and the fruit and the eater.

☆

In the 15th chapter of the Bhagavad-Gita Krishna says:

'I am the root of this great tree of the universe which has its beginning above in Me. The trees on earth get their nourishment from below and their form grows up, while this universal tree has roots above, in the Absolute; it gets its life-force from Him, and manifests as branches, leaves, fruits and flowers.'

The leaves are said to be the word or the sound. The individuals in the universe, in their varied forms, are nothing but sounds manifesting according to their nature and function. In nature a seed is the embodiment of some taste or smell which its fruit produced, while it holds the seed for further propagation. In the case of the great universal tree, the real seed is the Absolute which spreads out to manifest millions of forms, including all of us. In fact individuals also hold the same possibility, the taste of bliss which is in the original seed.

This is all we need to understand and live up to. The sap or the life-force of all forms is from the Absolute; Sat, Chit and Anand (Truth, Consciousness and Bliss). If one remembers this all the time, then one can act accordingly. People, when they see various forms around them, do not look beyond for the cause of all these forms. Reason, meditation and knowledge show that they all have their origin in the same single Absolute. Because people forget this fact, the teacher prescribes for them discipline, meditation, true knowledge. By attending to these one would soon learn to live this divine life within and without. One who remembers Absolute remembers Self, and he who is in the Self all the time is in the divine.

☆

The Absolute is the Atman of all and everything that exists, and one can see the repetition of it in every form and measure. We are in fact a duplicate in microcosm of the macrocosm. For instance, a surveyor prepares a map of a town and defines every road, lane and house. The map is a microcosm of the whole town and one can trace every detail of the town plan on the map. To know about the Absolute one should look to oneSelf. As above, so below. Everything shows the pattern of the Absolute.

The physical world, the universe, the whole of creation is the will of the Absolute. Everything is contained within Him. He is not contained within creation, but creation is contained within Him. He rules over everything. We are not contained in our body, although the individual lives in the body. Body is under the individual, the 'I', the Atman.

While Param-Atman is never in doubt, the individual always lives in doubt. Because of this he is always wanting miracles to happen in order to establish his faith. But even if a miracle does happen and his faith is established once, that faith is shaken again and again by subsequent doubts, and he wants fresh and repeated miracles to re-establish it. He fails to realize that he is constantly living in the midst of the most wonderful miracle, the world itself.

His own six-foot body is such a miracle that science can only wonder at it, without fully understanding or being able to make a single particle of it. The total market value of all the material in it (carbon, calcium etc.) is hardly worth four rupees, and yet what miracles are built out of it!

Again, it is in the very nature of the individual to be undergoing some change every moment. These changes continually lead him to a state of indecision and forgetfulness, so that he is never sure of himself. Thus he is unhappy. By contrast, one who has risen above his separate individuality is always sure of himself, never loses sight of his goal, and never changes it. We also should try to rise above our ego and to be in constant touch with the Param-Atman. Then we shall be happy, because unhappiness cannot exist with the Param-Atman. In fact, the thought of Param-Atman alone can dispel unhappiness immediately. For happiness, therefore, the shedding of the separate sense of 'I' is essential.

Q. If this tradition has existed for so long, why hasn't it produced more results?

H.H. Every spiritual truth, however simple, becomes distorted when it reaches an unrealized person. I will tell you a story.

A man went to a teacher and asked him about God, and the teacher said, 'I will answer your question in the simplest possible way, in three words—God is everywhere'. Well satisfied, for he felt that he now knew everything, the man went away. Going along the road he saw an elephant coming towards him with the mahout riding on its back and he thought to himself,

'God is everywhere, God is in the elephant, God is in me. Can God harm God? I will walk straight on', and when he got a little nearer the mahout first asked him to move out of the way and then shouted at him, but he said, 'No, God is in the elephant, God is in me, I am going on'. When he reached the elephant, the elephant took him in his trunk and threw him across the road, where he landed much shaken, bruised and damaged. So when he had recovered a little, he hobbled back to the teacher and said, 'I have been trying to act according to what you said and look what has happened to me', and the teacher said, 'Explain what happened'. He told the story, and the teacher said, 'You should understand fully before you begin to act. It is true that God is in everything—God was in the elephant, God was in you, but God was also in the mahout and the mahout told you to get out of the way. You disobeyed God and received what you deserved.'

Once an elephant appeared in a village; the news went around and everyone wanted to experience the elephant. Unfortunately most of the inhabitants were blind but still wanted to experience the elephant, so they had to be led to it. The mahout let them experience by touching the elephant, and of course each touched a different part. Then they met together to verify that they had experienced the real thing. The one who felt the foot said an elephant was a pillar, the one who had felt the tail said it was like a stick, and so it went on with the ears, trunk, tusks, fat belly etc. Each person described it according to the type of previous experience to which they could relate it. Then they started arguing. 'Yours was not the proper elephant, yours was illusion, mine is the only real one etc.' Later on the mahout told them, 'You cannot have a complete picture of the elephant. All you can do is put together all your different experiences of "elephant", and out of these experiences you can imagine a novel creature known as "elephant". But it is the sum of all these parts and something more, which represents the wholeness of the creature known as "elephant".'

In the same way, because of different quotations from the scriptures, it is possible for some sort of conflict or doubt to arise in the minds of people.

With the idea of enjoying the whole creation with an impartial attitude, one might ask where is the sense of being good, what is good and bad? The question never gets resolved. In fact there is neither good nor bad—it is simply our labelling. It is our preference for one or the other which makes one good and the other bad – our impertinence which makes one good and the other bad.

If one could keep to this state of silent impartial observer, one would see that none of these things exist. One stays in the present, and one acts as the occasion demands and the whole thing passes. Wise men once discussed this question of deriving happiness out of all the multifarious aspects of the world, and the discussion led to the conclusion that one should not entangle oneself with either side (physical or subtle), but should simply observe; because the Absolute is in everything, and this creation is a most efficient mechanical organism which is functioning according to the laws of the Absolute, so one should always see the Absolute behind all these passing phases.

Once Swami Rama Tirtha, who was from the Punjab, saw a black adder in his path; it was a puff adder with its hood open. He just smiled and laughed and said, 'Oh my God, you have come before me in such a frightening shape—but forgive me, I don't like your shape this time so please go away.' And the puff adder went away.

This shows how to behave as an unprejudiced and silent observer who has no duality (no mental division into 'good' and 'evil').

☆

Q. In the story of the man who ignored all the beautiful things offered, and would not buy anything, but only wanted to go and hold the king's hand, and buy that*, I have come to understand a little of what the king's right hand means, namely the Realised Man, and one clings to the Realised Man whenever possible.

H.H. The question of the right-hand man of the sovereign is very important because in fact when the sovereign shakes the hand, he withdraws, and gives away his own powers to the man who comes to shake hands with him. This is the unity of the Atman with the Param-Atman and it is a sort of test for anyone who wants to inherit the Kingdom of Heaven. Although it is open to anyone, what mostly happens is that people get bound to all the beautiful things provided by the Absolute. They start playing with them, accumulating them and keeping them, and as this goes on they forget that they have an appointment with the sovereign as well. They don't remember any more, so they don't

*See page 36

make any effort, but in the story there was one single man who did not avail himself of the celestial baths, the celestial food and dress, and all the riches made available. He went to the king and established his unity, inherited the kingdom and received the key and the power. Immediately he declared the rule of law, saying that this show had been put on to test the worth of the people, and those who were trying to take for themselves all the riches which had been made freely available to everyone were caught and put into prison. To be the right hand is to be the sovereign himself and the beauty of this is that such a man not only lives in the physical world with the best of laws and worship, but he can also return to unity with the Absolute whenever he feels the need for it.

Q. I now realise I have nothing of my own and that if I have some inner peace, the guidance comes. How to repay this vast debt? How to manifest the truth more in thought, word and action?

H.H. This realisation that 'I have nothing of my own' is the best realisation. This is the greatest achievement of evolution possible, because it signifies that the level of individual consciousness has been transcended into the universal level of consciousness. In this universal level, the universe as a whole gains predominant importance, and the importance of the individual is correspondingly reduced, but it also signifies that the whole universe is yours. The same has been explained in the Vedas. There are two chapters relating to this particular facet of knowledge—that the individual has nothing, and that the whole universe belongs to the individual. These chapters relate to two particular aspects of human consciousness. The first, which says 'there is nothing of my own' belongs to the feeling aspect of the individual, and the second which says 'the whole universe belongs to me' relates to the thinking aspect of human existence. In reality, there is no such division, but the realisation can only come through understanding of the apparent division. The effect is that one transcends the individual consciousness to the universal level. The physical effect of all this is that the individual becomes very light, the mind becomes very light and when it is very light, it becomes aware of creation as a whole.

This feeling of the realisation that 'there is nothing of my own' simply unites one in all respects with the universe. This does not in any way mean that there is nothing like the existence of the Self as well. The Self is there, but then it is united with the whole universe. Unless this realisation comes, one experiences the Self as opposed to the universe, so it comes about that there are two camps—one the individual, with his own existence on all levels; the other, apart from the individual, is the universe, and the individual has to communicate with the universe. But the realisation that 'there is nothing of my own' simply unites the individual Self with everything there is in creation.

Today, all of us need to understand and explain the Absolute, or Param-Atman, who is immanent, always present, together with us, guiding and helping, at each moment in every walk of life. We need to present this picture of the Absolute to ourselves and to others.

☆

Meditation, meditator, and the object of meditation—these three always go together. There can be no meditation if either the meditator or the object of meditation is not there. The object of meditation is Param-Atman, the ultimate truth, the absolute truth and the one and only truth that has real existence.

There is no such thing as the 'world' from the point of view of real existence. Yet we see a 'world' around us. This seeing is like seeing a mirage—seeing a thing where there is none.

Unreal though a mirage is, yet we cannot dispel it by any physical means. We cannot dig it out with a spade or blow it away with artillery. As it is due to certain conditions of light it goes away only when these conditions have gone. Similarly, the mirage of the 'world' is due to certain conditions of ignorance, and it goes away only when that ignorance is gone.

Consider a sugar cube; the real thing about it is its sweetness. Its form is irrelevant—whether it is cubical or round or any other shape. Now the Manas ('computer mind') is incapable of imagining 'sweetness', though it is real. It can, however, imagine objects having the property of sweetness, like the sugar cube or fruit or pudding; and these in turn enable us to realise what sweetness is. Thus to get at the abstract we take the help of the concrete; to get at the extra-sensory we go from the sensory object. Similarly we meditate with the help of a mantra, which is a sensation of sound, in order to get at something which is otherwise beyond the reach of the human mind—the Param-Atman.

We want to contemplate the Param-Atman. As it is the source of all greatness, its own greatness must be infinite. As it is the source of all happiness, its own happiness must be boundless. As it is the source of all beauty, its own beauty must be—we do not know. But how could we ever contemplate such a Param-Atman, whose qualities and nature are thus beyond the utmost stretch of human imagination?

This was the question which was put by Arjuna to the Lord Krishna, and the answer is contained in the Bhagavad-Gita, chapter 10, verses 20-42.

Here is a translation of a few of these verses:

'O Arjuna! I am the Self, seated in the hearts of all beings; I am the beginning and the life and I am the end of them all. . . .

Of the scriptures I am the hymns; I am the electric force in the powers of nature; of the senses I am the registering mind; and I am the intelligence in all that lives.

Among the vital forces I am life itself; I am Mammon to the heathen and godless; I am the energy in fire, earth, wind, heaven, sun, moon and planets. . . .

I am all-devouring death; I am the origin of all that may happen; I am fame, fortune, speech, memory, intellect, constancy and forgiveness.

I am the gambling of the cheat, and the splendour of the splendid; I am victory; I am effort; and I am the purity of the pure. . . .

Whatever is glorious, excellent, beautiful or mighty, be assured that it comes from only a part of My splendour.

But what is the use of all these details to you? O Arjuna! Enough that I sustain all this world with only a fragment of Myself!'

All this implies that by thinking of the most powerful manifest thing as only a tiny particle of Param-Atman's power; by thinking of the most beautiful object we can, and then treating it as a mere atom of Param-Atman's beauty and so on, we can gradually find our way to the Param-Atman. Thus, starting from sensory objects and rising higher and higher, we reach a state where all difference between sensory and ultra-sensory, between definable and indefinable has faded away from us.

Then, what to ordinary people are different forms and shapes are to a fully-realized person all manifestations of one and the same Param-Atman. What he sees then around himself and within himself is Param-Atman, and not the mirage which we call the 'world'. Such a man would welcome heat and cold, pleasure and pain, fortune and misfortune—all alike, because all are manifestations of Param-Atman.

☆

2 Who am I?

If you begin to be what you are, you will realise everything, but to begin to be what you are, you must come out of what you are not. You are not those thoughts which are turning, turning in your mind; you are not those changing feelings; you are not the different decisions you make and the different wills you have; you are not that separate ego. Well then, what are you? You will find when you have come out of what you are not, that the ripple on the water is whispering to you 'I am That', the birds in the trees are singing to you 'I am That', the moon and the stars are shining beacons to you 'I am That'. You are in everything in the world and everything in the world is reflected in you, and at the same time you are That—everything.

Q. What is Self-realization?
H.H. 'I am' and 'I am out of everything'. These are the two poles between which creation revolves. To realise this, that the creation is in myself and still I am out of it, is the sole purpose of Self-realization, to become only the observer, and allow everything to happen as it has to happen. One has to realise 'I am' before 'everything is'. Today I am in this puny form and yet have existed long before its creation, and also will live on when it is destroyed. To this vastness through eternity is the journey of Self-realization. Having a form and body, people come to limit the self to the body and the world

around without getting a glimpse of the vastness of eternity. Once you realize the greatness of what is not before you, then you find the right value of what does lie before you. To find this proper value is the work of Self-realization.

We live in the world of names and forms; we are surrounded by them, and even the being we call ourself has many names and forms. People have name and form, as well as the Atman; but because of ignorance people get involved in only the world of name and form. Usually they take their six-foot body as all they are. True knowledge and the method of meditation are to remove the narrowness of this boundary and bondage and allow people to discriminate and see the unlimited and unbounded Atman, which cannot be brought into the limits of names and forms. Here is an example:

Someone went to a holy man and asked to be introduced to God. The holy man said, 'When I go to Him, He will ask about you. What shall I say? First give me some details of your credentials'. The man pointed to his body and told his name. The holy man said, 'But that is made of flesh and bones and it is subject to growth and decay. How could this be you? It is only your body and name. Get me your proper credentials'. The man thought again and said that perhaps his thoughts, desires, feelings were his proper credentials. The holy man observed that these are changing all the time even more rapidly than the bodily form. 'Get me your true, fixed credentials', he asked.

In this way this man was led to recognize his own true Self, and then he did not go around seeking any more introductions.

☆

You cannot have complete happiness when you are limited, because there is still something left to desire. As long as the finite is not merged with the infinite, there will be desire, and so effort and prayer will be needed.

A person once came and asked, 'If God is omnipresent and omniscient, then whose ignorance is it?' The answer was, 'You are in truth omnipresent and omniscient, and ignorance is only forgetfulness'. So the ignorance belongs to the person who is asking the question.

☆

Q. At a certain stage in the development of meditation there seems to be a barrier blocking final unity. Is this illusion? If so, can one destroy it? If not, how can one overcome the barrier?

H.H. The last barrier to the Atman is ego, the feeling of 'I', I the one who is meditating, or I am the one who is about to go through the barrier into unity. As long as one sticks to this, unity is impossible. We have to learn this and make sure in ourselves that when we reach an obstacle of this nature, we should drop even the idea of the feeling of 'I'. Everything is to be given up, even the sense of 'I'. Once the sense or feeling of 'I' is given up, only then is unity possible.

A certain man went to a holy man to be initiated in

meditation. He was asked what things he had seen on the way. He said the one thing he remembered seeing was a donkey. He was then asked to remove it from his memory. The poor man tried hard, but had to admit that he could not do it. The holy man said that the art is to drop the memory. This memory or the feeling of 'I' is the greatest and the last barrier to meditation. The man who meditates or the man who observes must be dropped so that he is able to merge into one.*

All claims of being the doer of actions or enjoyer of objects relate to ego. When wisdom dawns, then the distinction between the witness and doer becomes clear and one understands that one is the witness and not the doer or enjoyer. This witness is the stillness; the claims of doing and enjoying are the din of the market, the realm of movement, the place of businessmen. In the Gita Lord Krishna says, 'The fool, whose mind is deluded by egoism, considers himself to be the doer.'

As long as there is the feeling of doing and achieving, the individual is in the movement and not in stillness.

If one hangs a coat in the wardrobe, the inanimate coat can't put itself on anyone's body. It will remain where it is. When you put it on, it goes with you everywhere. So it is with the body. The body is the coat; if you claim the body as your own, then it accompanies you everywhere, but as soon as you stop claiming, then it takes its proper place as part of nature. Then the 'I' becomes the witness, having no attachment.

When one is on the road one may call for a taxi, but the taxi and the driver are different and the call is

*See page 49

answered by the driver and not by the taxi. Thus, when we are called by some name, it is the name of the body but people take it for the Self. When by reason one learns to differentiate between the body and the spirit, then all these claims of being the doer or the enjoyer do not matter. Then all pains and pleasures of body and mind, though they still remain, do not torment or overwhelm.

☆

Q. Would H.H. please say how the daily activities of a job in life can be brought more under the influence of Sattva? There are rare and wonderful times when a feeling of only being the instrument in trying to help people is felt. How to make these more frequent?

H.H. Suppose one is engaged in caring for infants or small children, there is never a sense of duty, work, service, obligation, help, sacrifice or any other form of ego, for it is only play. This play is due to love. There is nothing beside love; no idea of personality or ego arises from either side.

This is real work. Here persons are only instruments and the creation is bliss. If one could establish the same relationship in daily work, then the doer is an instrument and the receiver is also an instrument, and the two Atmans become One. The unity thus achieved becomes a fountain of happiness. We all experience such moments of joy when we remove our covers of individuality or personality or any type of ego. The remedy is simple. Give up all idea of being the doer and it will all be bliss everywhere.

☆

One of the fundamental characteristics of worldly life is the illusion of being the independent doer—of having free will. It is very difficult to maintain that individuals are the doers of anything, for the whole creation is a manifestation of the Absolute who is the real doer. He has made His whole show in such a beautiful pattern that keeps changing from one moment to another, and it must also keep on multiplying. The whole thing is going on by virtue of the creative impulse given by the Absolute; He is the independent one, He is the free one, and He is the real doer.

Part of the show is our human nature with its capacities of memory and thinking. If one takes the load of the 'past' and the 'future' upon oneself, the journey becomes hard and treacherous; 'past' and 'future' appear terribly big, and it is very difficult to walk along the path if one carries this load. 'If I had done such and such', one thinks, 'then this or that could have been achieved'; or, 'if I hadn't acted as I did, all this trouble could have been avoided'. One should always keep oneself light-hearted and free of this burden.

In fact, the load is on the mind, the physical body has nothing to do with it; but because the mind governs the physical body, the physical body also suffers.

One of the best analogies is the shadow play of puppets. There is someone holding the strings and moving them, but they appear to be moving themselves and to be the real doers.

The whole of creation is very much like a puppet show, with the strings being held by somebody else.

Take the example of a cinema show, where the film is being shown on the screen and the people keep on looking at these moving pictures. On the screen you see mountains, buildings, seas, and fights, love scenes and religious scenes. All types of scene are being enacted on this screen. Some people watching are like the puppets, and they get animated by the scenes. One should be able to see the things which are happening in the world—but only as a silent observer. See all the pleasures on the screen, but don't get involved and moved off course.

How can anyone else judge the Self? If someone knows, then he never asks anyone's approval. Self-realization can't be proved by certificates, recommendations or affirmations by anyone else. When the Self knows itself to be free, only then is it free. If anyone pretends to be free, then he is only deceiving himself, not realizing.

Self-realization is by the Self. The test of all work and use of all discipline, knowledge and devotion is only this, and when the disciple comes to the point where he sees himself in the light of truth, then he knows that 'he knows'. Then there is nothing more to ask, nothing left to achieve.

Everyone experiences unity with the Atman but does not know it. During deep sleep the self merges with the universal Self. This happens in ignorance but is a natural phenomenon. If during active life or meditation one does not feel this merging, it is because of a sheath. This sheath is natural too. The unity which is experienced is the light thrown by the Atman on this sheath. If the sheath is transparent and pure, then all is well, but if it is cloudy or dirty, one only gets a glimmer. This is the brink of direct experience. If the water in the Ganges were universal Atman, then water taken from the Ganges and put into a bottle would be the individualised self, although the water is the same. Once you open or break the bottle letting the water flow back into the Ganges, you would no longer see any difference, and the water could not be taken back for it would have merged with the Ganges again for ever. The only thing that made it different is the sheath which separates the individual Atman from the universal Atman.

Q. What is the purpose of the bottle?

H.H. The Creator created the universe in all its different aspects and forms. He observes the drama which he has created. All who take part in this play and know its mystery and essence are detached. They play their part and enjoy it. Those who do not know its mystery become identified with their parts and are bound by them. When they lose their identification they too can enjoy playing their part in the grand drama without being bound.

A man from the country was visiting his relatives in the city. To entertain him, they took him to the cinema. They bought expensive seats in the back row, but their country cousin was insulted at being put at the back. He insisted that they sit in the very front. All went well until suddenly a lion appeared on the screen, and looked as if it would jump at the audience. The visitor took his stick and struck at the lion to defend himself. The screen was broken, the film stopped and the place was thrown into darkness and confusion. At first no one could understand what had happened; then they realised that in the audience was a man who had never been to a cinema before and took the film to be real.*

The same applies to those ignorant people who regard what goes on in the world as real and become identified and involved, leading to foolish actions; when the real significance of the grand drama is known, these people can play their part with detachment and enjoyment.

One starts the mantra, and repeats the mantra. One initiates this at the level of the individual, and then this repetition of the mantra leads on to the bare thread of meditation.

Although it is known as the 'practice of meditation', yet this practice is leading towards the end of all activity. Slowly and gradually this march towards non-activity takes place until one reaches the realm of unity and stillness. This is the experience of Self as universal; here there is no duality and there remains no place to move on to, and there is no time to change to for He is the place, the time and also the substance. In that profound silence, stillness or union all movements stop; there is only 'One without a second' and that is Atman Himself, the Observer.

*See page 27

3 Waking

Knowledge is the same everywhere in the Absolute and in Atman. Atman's knowledge of the Absolute is direct. As true knowledge is stored in the Absolute, Atman has direct access to it. However, when we become too involved in worldly activities and ambitions, we forget about that true knowledge. Eventually the habits arising from this involvement create clouds which block out true knowledge altogether. Then we have no access to it. When we come across someone who has that access, our memory is stirred and we remember true knowledge. Once that memory is stirred it is impossible to forget in this life. One will always remember that true knowledge is there, and it is up to one whether to take it or not. For example if you stand under a tree on a river bank and look at the water, you feel that you are moving but a glance at the bank will show you that it is the water and not you that is moving. In the same way, if we get involved in worldly things, we come to think that it is they which are stable, whereas, if we have an observer, a glance inwards will show that it is we ourselves, the Atman, which is stable while the worldly things are moving.

Vyasa says, 'I have made a critical study of the scriptures several times. The gist of all that, as I found, is that we should think of the Param-Atman all the time'. As soon as any other thought enters the mind, we are in the grip of Maya or illusion, which catches hold of us and takes us very far away.

The individual or our Self is a part of the Param-Atman, and it has come into the world for the sake of discovering joy. But, instead of that, it has fallen into the trap of ignorance. Ignorance is forgetting the reality. It is the root cause of all the troubles associated with the world. Therefore the biggest of all the troubles is to forget the reality. And, by forgetting the reality, we mean forgetting that only Param-Atman is real and the sensory world is unreal.

A schoolboy was given a new penknife by his parents for his birthday, and he took it to school with him. Usually he carried his penknife in his satchel, but that day he wore the new one in his belt. But when he wanted it, he forgot that it was in his belt and searched for it again and again in the satchel. Not finding it, he thought his classmates had stolen it, and reported the theft to the teacher. The whole class was punished. This is how a most ordinary instance of forgetting causes big trouble.

All worldly objects are like children's toys—a toy elephant, a toy motor car, a toy locomotive etc. They must be treated as nothing more than toys. Disappointments and trouble will be our lot if we treat them as real. All troubles which we encounter in our life are due to treating the world as real.

The first of the Upanishads begins, 'Whatever lives is full of the Lord. Claim nothing; enjoy, do not covet His property. Then hope for a hundred years of life doing your duty'. They do not ask us to live a hundred years of misery. However, our life can become a life of misery because of our feeling of attachment to worldly objectives, and this attachment to worthless things is the root of all miseries. The world, as it really is, has no miseries at all. It is we who manufacture them by harbouring an attachment to worldly objects.

Attachment means, to consider as ours what really belongs to God. Our body, our house, our wealth, our son etc. Give up this feeling, and you get rid of all troubles.

A baby cannot eat solid food in the beginning because the ability has not been acquired. But this ability comes quite easily later when he tries (after he has some teeth!). Acquiring the ability to think of the Param-Atman is as easy as that.

Do not think that the world around you—your house, your money, your body—are insubstantial. Rather, it is your feeling of attachment to them that is insubstantial. Whatever is happening around you is right, but what is wrong about it is the view you are taking of it. If you could correct your viewpoint, you would be happy.*

The world is a great show, which God is staging around you in the shape of the universe. But it is a mere show. Your birth is a show, your death is a show. Actually there is neither birth nor death. Know that, and you would be happy.

The common outlook is that the world is everything, and that Param-Atman is nothing. It is a crime to hold this view, and the punishment for it is to be imprisoned in this physical body. You cannot be happy while undergoing a term of imprisonment.

Our mind has the property of thinking of something or other all the time; it cannot remain idle. If it does not remember the Param-Atman, it would think of the

*See page 139

world. Remembering the Param-Atman leads to happiness, and thinking of the world leads to unhappiness.

It is true that people do not find it easy to hold the Param-Atman in mind. The reason for that is lack of practice. As long as the ability has not been acquired, there would be difficulty. But ability can certainly be acquired.

You have a mind, you have a body, and you have intelligence. Let the mind be trained to remember the Param-Atman, let the body do service to Him, and let the intelligence discriminate.

Once there was a king who felt the need of a saint, but there wasn't one around, so he sent a minister and servants to search everywhere. They combed all the forests and found various hairy men, supposed to be holy, but they couldn't find a real saint. In desperation, after the first month of the three allotted to them, the minister said to one of his servants, 'There's nothing for it, you'll have to do it. You'll have to sit meditating and perhaps in two months you'll look the part, and anyway some hair will grow on your head and chin!'

The servant did this and the king came and recognized him as holy and bowed down to him. The situation thus having been saved, the minister said to the servant, 'Well done! Now have a haircut and get back to your job, serving me'. But the servant said, 'No, I don't serve you any more. While I was meditating I discovered what I really wanted and now I'm going for that alone'.

☆

Love is the motive force behind all the processes at work in the world to sustain it. It could never be sustained without love. In the case of human life, its examples are the love of parents, the love of brothers, the love of friends and colleagues etc. Even the behaviour of insects and moths seem to be based on some form of love. So much so, that the ultimate cause of hostility is also love, because hostility springs up when love is hindered. Thus a duality of love and hostility prevails everywhere. We want a thing we love; if we do not get it, we turn hostile.

A love free from the above duality is true love. The whole drama enacted by Param-Atman depicts this one thing only. But there is none to understand it.

A perennial game of hide-and-seek seems to be going on. We are all seeking something. Some seek it in annihilation, some in creation, some in light, some in darkness, some in intellect, etc. Actually it is Param-Atman that all are seeking, and Param-Atman is hidden in all these and in everything else. But while seeking people have forgotten what it is that they are seeking.

A man wanted to go to his father-in-law's place to meet his wife. He went to the railway station where the train was standing at the platform, and he shouted at the booking clerk, 'A ticket to my father-in-law's place, please!'

'Where on earth is that?' asked the booking clerk.

'Oh, my father-in-law's place! Please! Please! Quick!'

'Just tell me the name of the place'.

'I'm telling you, my father-in-law's place. For God's sake be quick! The train is about to leave!'

And the train started, leaving the man behind.

Something like that is happening to all of us.

☆

Maharshi Raman went on meditating for fourteen years over the question: 'Who am I?' As soon as he was on the right path, it took him only a minute to realize that he was everything.

This is what is happening with all of us. In a state of continual confusion we have been searching for something without finding it. We want to know what we are. We want to be happy. That is, we are seeking Param-Atman. But Param-Atman is sitting in every-thing, though there is a curtain of ignorance between Him and us.

We should see Param-Atman in everything. If we do that, we receive special favours from Him. Then this curtain of ignorance lifts and the illusory world of Maya—which has been cheating us all the time— no longer does so and begins to help us instead.

☆

There was a king who organised a great universal exhibition. He invited exhibits from all over the world, and stalls of beautiful things were arranged in this exhibition. People assembled there to buy whatever pleased them. There was one particular man who used to move round the stalls and examine them intimately, and yet he bought nothing. He went round day after day. People wondered why this man kept on looking at things but never bought anything. They tried to persuade him but he said he would only buy when something really satisfied him. When only two days remained some people reminded him he had very little time left—he had better make his choice quickly, otherwise he would lose the chance of buying anything at all. He said he wanted to wait to see what really pleased him. This went on till at the last moment when the stalls were about to be closed for ever, he went to the king who organised it all, and he held the king's hand. He said, 'This hand has organised such a beautiful exhibition, I want to buy it', and he asked the price. The king said it was difficult to imagine that he himself was on sale, or that his hand could be for sale! There were other things to be bought but not the king. But the man said, 'It is you who have brought about such beauty so I want you, not the things'. The king said, 'If you really want me you can have me only by love, not by money.' So the man said he was prepared and he surrendered himself with great devotion to the king, and then because he surrendered himself he won the king and then all the things in the exhibition which belonged to the king belonged to him. He had no reason to buy anything because everything was now his own. He could use whatever he wanted whenever he wanted; he did not have to claim, he did not have to collect. It is only by surrender to the Absolute through love that one wins all. That is the way we need to go.*

Dr. R. Everybody wants to know why this has to be at the last possible moment, just before closing time?

H.H. Although things are usually recognised only at the last moment, this does not mean that they were not there all the time. In the beginning everybody knew this, and everybody loved, but in course of time this love is lost, this devotion is lost, and now the search has started. This happens with ordinary things in one's house. People have their things, but somehow they get lost, and they have to keep searching until they find

*See page 16

them. Once they are rediscovered people seem to enjoy, in a mysterious way, the belief that they have now got them, although in fact it was only ignorance which made it difficult to trace the things, which were in their house all the time. Things are never lost—nothing is lost—it is only through ignorance or forgetfulness that we seem to have lost them.

☆

The whole thing is that we never remember ourSelves. All our troubles come from not remembering ourSelves, only we can't talk about this because it is never understood. You have to reach realization before you can understand it. I will tell you a story:

Ten men were sitting on the Ganges bank, as we are sitting now, and they decided to swim across to the other side. On the way over they got nervous because of the current, so, when they came to the other side, they began to count heads. They counted up and, to their horror, found there were only nine and, whoever counted, the answer was always nine. They almost began to prepare for the funeral but the tenth man was always himself (the man who was counting), and always forgotten, not counted.

Only this is difficult to understand. It is as if each of us possessed two houses. One is a tiny little house, nothing in it, bars on the windows, and in that house we live all our lives. We forget that we also possess a magnificent house, full of costly rugs and furniture, everything we could want, servants at our command. If we could only remember that we owned also this other house, we would not be content with living in the little house all the time. When we start to meditate we gradually come out of the little house and we sit for a time between the two houses. When we transcend everything that belongs to our personal life and reach the stage of absolute silence, we are sitting between the two houses without yet realizing the big spacious house. If we come out of the little house often enough, and sit for long enough, the memory of the big and spacious house will begin to come to us; we will begin to walk there; we will get a glimpse of it; we will be able to go in. Once we realize what a wonderful house it is, we will never want to go back to the little house. So, memory of this great big house is self-remembering, but it is not the same as realization. Self-remembering is remembering the existence of this big house; realization is when you go in and live there.

Q. 'Before we could know who we are, we have to learn to come out of what we are not'. We have begun to see some of the things we are not, but how can we begin to see what we are?

H.H. Whenever one has lost something in the physical sense one has to get some light to look for it. Many different types of light could be used—a small lamp, a lantern, electric light, moonlight and sunlight. They are sufficient for the physical world.

In the subtle world, if one has lost anything there, one has to get the light of knowledge, the light of the subtle world, and with that light one can find what one has lost. As far as the Self is concerned, the Self is always experienced by everyone whether one is lost in the physical darkness, or within the subtle darkness of ignorance. In each case the Self is always experienced and present—one does not need any other agency to find out the Self and experience the Self, and no one can deny the existence of the Self, because there is no other means of denying it except the Self! The situation is that the Self is always available and whatever is available and experienced does not need any extra light. The light we need is only on the physical and subtle levels. For that we can take the physical light or the subtle light of knowledge from the scriptures, from a Realized Man, or Teachers. Even with knowledge, if the knowledge is not complete, we still cannot transcend the subtle world and in that way transcend to the reality beyond this subtle world, so the proper experience of the Self is not constant and continuous. The Self is eternal and the Self is the light of lights. The Self is consciousness, and the Self is happiness. It is eternal and it is truth, and none of these things can be lost because they are ever-present everywhere. One has simply to dispel the physical darkness or the subtle darkness which is prevailing, because the Self is always with each of us. Let the Self prevail. There is no need to search for it.

☆

We have to cleanse our inner being. There is dirt there due to the Gunas—Sattva, Rajas and Tamas.* We remove this dirt by providing light. What is this light? Is it the light of the sun, the moon, electric light, or something like that? No, none of them. The light is the light of Atman.

We can see the image of the sun in the water, but

*Gunas: See page 72

when there are ripples in the water, then the image appears to quiver. The quivering is in the water, not in the sun.

If the water is muddy the image is not clear, but the dirt exists in the water, not in the sun.

What are the methods of purifying and clearing our inner body? I will explain in detail, though some are already well known. Good action, holy action, holy thought and service, considering everybody to be part of the same Param-Atman, treating other people as our own selves. Remembering that the same pure Param-Atman permeates all the living beings that we come across, as a universal brotherhood. These provide the light with which we are purified within.

Sun, moon, fire, electricity are four sources of light. A fifth source is knowledge, which activates everything. It is not a physical light like the light emitted by the sun, moon etc, but it is a thing which enables us to know. We can call the light of knowledge a light but it is unlike the light we get from the sun. It is simply that which enables us to know.

Knowledge has two faces—one is yes, the other is no. Acceptance/rejection. Whether it is so or whether it is not so. If we sit in a completely dark room where we can see nothing, we shall still see one thing and that is our own Selves, the Atman. Sitting in a dark room that which knows 'I am here', that is knowledge. That knowledge has to be joined up with the physical light by which we see. The joining of these two results in our worldly progress.

The eye by itself cannot see anything; there must be light, the brain, and the intention of seeing the thing we are looking at. We may be looking at a thing and not be seeing it. We can also see a thing but not understand it.

Seeing and understanding both become possible with knowledge—consciousness.

Knowledge is the giver of light to light. It provides light to worldly light but even if there is no worldly light, the light of knowledge still exists.

An individual is working for Self-realization. The Realized Man looks at it differently. He knows that there is nothing like Self-Realization. The Self is itself real. Who can make it real? What one is really doing is trying to remove the cloud of ignorance. The eye can see perfectly well under the sunlight. If there is a cloud in between, the vision becomes dim; the thicker the cloud, the dimmer the vision. The eye is like the Atman, the sun is like the Absolute and ignorance is the cloud. This is the barrier. Eye and sun are made of the same element. The more one gets light, the more darkness disperses. Moon gives more light than lamps; sun gives more light than moon. Two suns will give more light than one, and so on. When one gets the light of the Atman, which is the Absolute, then even the suns become brighter. That is when the unity is seen. The unity is there, the Self which is real is all there; it is only a matter of enlightenment.

By discrimination we get liberation. Bondage is by ignorance.

Here is an illustration:

If a coiled piece of rope is lying where there is not enough light, one may think it is a snake. Then with the thought that it is a snake there comes a fear of death, but that can be removed by a flood of light—this knowledge that it is not a snake.

When by the light of discrimination one understands that this is not real, and that it is all a manifestation of God himself—the Lord Almighty—then one knows that everything is God himself. All that we can see is not the world but God himself.

The light of the Atman is eternal and embraces everything. Once this connection with the all-pervading light is established, one knows everything. This is the light of true knowledge, the consciousness. Where there is light, there can't be darkness. No one can trace darkness when possessed of light. One whose clouds are dispersed with the wind of discipline so that the connection with the light is established, he sees all—within and without. Everyone feels his own existence, but an ordinary man can only feel the body and some of its reactions, whereas a conscious man comprehends more than the eye can see. That is because of the light of consciousness.

☆

4 Meditation

Meditation is meant for the realization of the chief aim of human life. The coarse material world of our sense organs and the pleasure it gives, do not fulfil this aim, so we need something besides. The reason for discontent is that the world of pleasure is small and temporary compared with the divine Self or Atman. It is a law that the small cannot satisfy the large; the large needs satisfaction comparable with its own magnitude and permanence. Atman is eternal and complete, but the visible tangible world is not. But when in their ignorance people call their body 'I' (mistaking the body for the real 'I' or Atman), they find it difficult to derive full satisfaction, peace and lasting happiness. And then they turn their minds to look for things which could lead to such a result. There are many ways to achieve this, but this system of meditation is simple and easy and can be practised while remaining in the world of normal life. That is why the ordinary man needs this meditation.

Where did the meditation come from? The Creator begins the act of creation with meditation. The meditation is from the beginning of creation and will only end with creation. Although history is very long, yet at least one should know that meditation alone was the means of creation. The Creator meditates to create, and also meditates to bring about modifications. This is the means of creative activity. If men meditate they switch on, or tune into the creative force, and find enough power to do their daily activities, and prepare for union with the eternal Self as well. Meditation is like light vibrations which are everywhere at all times. Those few people with cosmic consciousness catch it by inspiration and pass it on to others to help them become connected with the creative force.

(H.H. nodded assent when told that part of his answer reminded the listener of the first words of the Gospel of St. John: 'In the beginning was the Word, and the Word was with God and the Word was God.... All things were made by Him...')

The sound of a festival in an Indian village seems like a roar from a distance, but once you get there the roaring sound seems to disappear because you become part of it. Likewise during meditation the distracting noises seem very harsh, but if one expands oneself so as to cover everything, then these distractions become very minor things, for they are part of yourself. One would notice them but is not disturbed.

In the same way when anything passes by another object at great speed, it seems that both are moving. Trains are examples. People sitting in a moving train have the impression that the motionless train is also moving, but in fact it is not. If you are in the motionless train and take no notice of the moving train, then you feel motionless, but the moment your attention is drawn towards the moving train you also get the illusion of movement. The same happens in meditation. If you attend to interference, it starts interfering; if you don't, you are safe.

The Absolute is motionless, but his ray of creation is

full of motion. Although all motion is his own creation, he never gets involved in it. In meditation the Atman can also be surrounded by moving interference and still he can remain detached and motionless. The Absolute recharges the energy of the universe by dissolving it. We get recharged with energy by sleep at night. This recharges the physical body, but in meditation, in deep rest and peace, we also recharge the whole being and not only the body....

Music has the power to give bliss because the vibrations emanating from rightly composed notes form certain patterns of particles which create bliss....

Everything is vibration. In vibrations live all words and knowledge.

☆

The ultimate end of the meditation is to reach to total immobility, or the profound stillness, and this is very deep. No meter could measure it; it is without end. It is unnecessary to remain in this state for a long period. Longer meditation does not necessarily achieve this profound stillness.

Those who manage to dive deep, come out with potentiality emanating from the will of the Absolute.

In the Mahabharata, Arjuna asks Shri Krishna about the man with such stillness. In the Gita, such a man is called Sthitaprajna—'one who is steady and still in his knowledge and being'. Krishna says that such a man would not be agitated in discomfort, pain or misery. He would not rise in revolt against such misfortune. Even if a calamity befalls, he neither gives up nor feels sorry—he only attends to overcoming its effects with a smile. When honoured with success, pleasure, or comforts he never bursts into jubilation; he simply accepts them with gratitude, and then forgets. In short, one could say that a man with this profound stillness always remains the same and expresses efficiency, wisdom, love and mercy.

Q. That proves that this immobility or stillness must be ever present; therefore, it would seem that meditation starts there?

H.H. One would say rather that this stillness is itself the real experience of meditation. Since there is no movement, one cannot call it a starting point—for nothing is 'starting'. When one comes out of such a state, then one comes out with the treasure, and this treasure is without end. In ordinary rest and stillness one regains only some of one's lost energy; but, having reached this stillness, one is never without energy and love. Such a man always does everything fresh, new and for the first time. This is because his sensations, movements, instincts and emotions come together in unity to face any situation. When he tackles any problem, all his forces work through this one-pointed attention.

Meditation is the process to take one from movement to non-movement. As long as there is any appreciation of sound or smell or any other sense, then one is still separated from the immobile substance. That substance is there and in true meditation one becomes that substance.

However subtle a sound may be, it exists because of

the movement, and as long as there is movement, there is separation. Thus the climax of meditation is that one becomes One. There is nothing else. Only 'One without a second'.

Q. There is still some confusion at home about the word 'deep'. People think it has to be in coarse form, placed anatomically, whereas it surely means deep in a subtle way—deep into your being?

H.H. In both ways analogy can explain the subject very well. One can take the analogy of the ocean; one dives deep, and as one goes deeper and deeper one finds stability, for the bottom of the sea is stable compared with the surface. Throughout the universe the less mobile supports the more mobile and then the more mobile supports the super-mobile. The whole of nature is mobile and is supported by the immobile Creator. In nature everything is supported by something else. The moving earth, for instance, is immobile in relation to mobile man on the street. In the Vedas it is said that three-fourths of the Absolute is immobile and one-fourth is mobile. Thus in meditation 'to go deep' means to go from mobility to immobility.

There is a story about a flock of crows. One of them was strong, clever and good looking, so they made him their leader. This king of the crows felt proud of his exploits, and looked down upon all other creatures.

One day a young swan appeared. The crows assembled around the swan and asked him if he knew about the great deeds of their king. He pleaded ignorance and wished to see their king. The king crow appeared and asked the swan about different types of flight. The swan, in his simplicity, said that he knew only one style.

The king crow then embarked on an exhibition of his hundred-and-one styles of flight. Having performed his acrobatics, he asked to see the art of the swan. The young swan took off in a graceful, gentle and natural flight and, as usual, increased his speed only gradually. Since the crow was small and swift he flew fast, and realizing that the swan was left behind, he came back to cheer him up. The swan gradually increased his speed, and it was not very long before the crow was tired and trembled, and eventually fell into the sea. The swan came down and rescued the crow and helped him back to his flock. The crow then became ashamed of his pride, and thanked the swan for his modesty and magnanimity. You see, the swan lived a natural life, while the crow occupied himself in acrobatics and cleverness.

The ultimate victory goes to the natural, steady, still and simple man; while the clever and smart waste their energy in trifling pursuits that only lead to their destruction.

Somebody once went to a Realized Man and asked to be given the meditation. The Master asked him, 'As you were coming to me, what did you see on the way?' He remembered only that there was a donkey lying on the road. The Master said, 'All right! I will give you one little exercise, and if you can do that, then I will give you the system of meditation. Just go and sit quietly and get that

donkey out of your mind. Take your time and come
back when you've done it! The poor man tried for two
hours, but he found that the memory of the donkey
became only clearer and clearer; he couldn't get the
donkey out! After two hours he was in despair and
came to the Master and said, 'I'm extremely sorry, but
that donkey is not getting out of my mind at all!' The
Realized Man said, 'Listen! You saw that donkey only
once, yet you couldn't lose him even after two hours.
Now there is a mass of stuff that you have collected in
your mind throughout the ages. In life after life you
have collected all this, and it will be much more difficult
to get rid of all that you have been living with, than to
remove something you just saw once! So you can't
expect to lose it all in a few days. If you understand that,
you will realize that discipline is necessary. If you are
determined and really want to get rid of that burden,
you will have to be quiet and have patience. From your
experience with the donkey you must first realize that
you must not try to get rid of anything! Don't fight with
your desires; don't try to push them out; don't try to
settle them. But just be carefree about them; get the
'couldn't care less' attitude. Just lose them, neglect
them, and they will go away one by one. Don't struggle
with them. I tell you that it is the only way it can be
done.'*

☆

The whole universe is divided in two—I and the rest!
This is the world of division and we live in this world of
duality. The method of meditation is to lead us from
duality to unity. This method is not the end. It is like a

*See page 25

rope through which we can go into the well or come out. Once the necessary job is accomplished, it is left behind. The mantra is not unity, it only leads to unity where the world of division has no validity. This unity is the Absolute, known as Truth, Consciousness and Bliss. Once we reach there, a miraculous alchemy takes place, and the being is charged with energy just as one gets a car battery charged for further use. If, in meditation, after sounding the mantra, we start looking for anything, maybe a sound or substance, we undo the meditation. Even talking of 'appreciation' is duality. In deep meditation we don't even appreciate the peace, truth, bliss or consciousness; we in fact become peaceful, truthful, blissful and conscious of the Self. One must give up all ideas of appreciating anything about the mantra. This is exactly opposite to what meditation stands for. Start the mantra and do nothing but follow the mantra. The mantra will naturally settle down into that unity where there is no activity and no division.

The achievement of physical stillness is in itself no ordinary thing; it is a very important achievement. Three factors come together in meditation—the body, the eyes and the mind. When the body is totally still, the next movement is found in the eyes; they will keep on flickering, however slight this may be. When the eyes are still, the mind will follow suit. Mind moves in response to the movement of the body. Stillness of the body first, then of the eyes, is followed by peacefulness of the mind.

Meditation, as it has been given to you, starts with the body, and the training of the body to become still is the first stage of entry into the spiritual world. Once that has been achieved, there is not much difficulty in achieving the stillness of the mind in due course.

The sage who wrote the Mandukya Upanishad (Mandukya means 'frog') said that with 'three jumps' one can get into the deepest level of the Self, just as a frog who happens to be on dry land and is getting scorched by the sun, and wants to be cool and peaceful, can with three jumps enjoy the cool and peace of the deepest water. Similarly, these are the three jumps we need, and by means of them it should be possible to establish the stillness of the mind.

☆

Q. Could H.H. say more about how to still the mind when the body is totally still in meditation?

H.H. The relation of mind to body is already established and strong; nothing is independent, and everything starts with the body. If the body is still, there is no reason at all why the mind should not be still. So if the mind is not still, the only conclusion is that the body has not yet become totally still—there must be some movement in the body which has yet to be stilled. Once it is totally still, then you will find the mind surrenders its movement and becomes still.

Q. On an earlier occasion His Holiness said you could not tailor your physical body, but that you could tailor your subtle or mental level, but only by going to the spiritual level, and that, once you pronounced the mantra properly, the process was 'automatic'. Can we know more about this 'automatic' process and whether faith is needed that it is going on even if one does not recognise deep peace?

H.H. In situations where mind does not become still one can put a resolution to the mind that we are not to be disturbed when meditation is going on—so (to the mind) 'I delegate you to be the gatekeeper of my inner body. You stay there and do not let any movement take place in the body, in the eyes, and do not allow any thoughts to come into me, because I am going to be busy with the Self'. Put a resolution, make a resolution, delegate the mind, and see that the job which has been given is carried out by the mind—let it do this job! If it does stand at the gate of the inner being it will be doing the job properly and you will not be troubled. This is a resolution which you have to give to your mind.

When one sits for meditation in a still position, there may be distractions outside and these distractions will attract the mind. One has to learn not to be distracted by outer influences.

Apart from outer distractions, there are internal riots! These keep going in the mind; it keeps returning to certain things which one wants to do—it is simply presenting different 'files' for your consideration! When you are almost still, you can give more energy to these files, so your mind tries to get you to look at them. In fact, this is not the time for them, so make a resolution—tell the mind this is not the time for those files—'When I have finished my meeting with the Self, then I will surely attend to them!' You attend to those files later, resolving those questions which seem to be bothering the mind. This is the way—order him—he will follow your commands provided you do command. Make a resolution, let him stay at the gate, and ask him not to allow any files to be presented to you because this is not the time. You will see them later on. And do see them later on.

Someone in pursuit of spiritual knowledge and practice turned to some sort of rituals in order to gain control of a ghost. He hoped to get most of his work done by this ghost so that he would be free himself to meditate, study and do spiritual work. So he gained control of the ghost in order to use it like a servant. But this ghost was very powerful and very quick to complete the tasks, and then returned for more orders. Before the ghost had taken on the job, it had said that, if there was no work, it would devour the man! This was the condition—it must be kept busy all the time! This man thought there was so much to do that the ghost could be kept busy like a human being, but the ghost was so fast that very soon it finished all the work the man could think of. Now the man had an inspiration. He realized that the ghost was so quick that it could never be given enough jobs, so it should be given some job it must attend to all the time and that would never come to an end. He told the ghost to cut a bamboo pole and bring it to him. He asked the ghost to fix the bamboo pole in the courtyard. When the ghost had fixed it firmly there, the man said, 'Unless I ask you to come and do a special job, your general job is to go up and down this pole!' Going continually up and down this pole exhausted the ghost very quickly, and then it settled down at the bottom of the pole to wait for the next order from this holy man!*

Mind is very like a ghost; its job is to propose and counter-propose and there is no end to the variety of counter-propositions it can produce. This is the job of the mind, and that is how it keeps people busy, and people get tired, not only mentally but physically.

Whether the meditation is working properly or not, only the individual can be the best judge. He will know what is happening within himself, and one knows that there will be difficulties which will be resolved only in the course of time. Unless the meditation has become natural with the individual, he will have to continue to meet difficulties. Sometimes there are more, sometimes less and sometimes they do not arise at all.

One never encounters difficulties all the time, because they arise from the influx of the Gunas. When Rajas is predominant, one may find that one cannot meditate. Under Tamas one may feel sleepy or there may be a hundred-and-one different types of hindrances. We can welcome the hindrances and let them come, but on one basic condition, namely, that we are completely resolved to go on the way of meditation and to achieve the object of meditation—have union with this unchanging Param-Atman, the Absolute. With this, let us journey on. Whatever comes, we accept it and keep on doing the best we can.

*See page 87

To meditate is to be. To be One. One without a second. Here is an example: In ancient times Dattatreya was walking along a street and a marriage procession came by. He stopped at the door of a shop where arrows were being made. The arrowmaker was busy at his work and did not bother to look at the procession. After it had passed, Dattatreya wanted to know why the man had not enjoyed the merry procession. He asked if he had seen it. The arrowmaker said no. He said that he had not heard anything because he was busy shaping the point of the arrow. In shaping the point he became one with it, and the world of senses did not exist for him at that time. The same applies to meditation. In meditation one is just One. One becomes the Self. The method of meditation is only a process by which this is made possible. Absolute meditates and becomes the creation; we meditate and become the Absolute.

There are three types of rest: the bodily rest of the physical realm, the mental rest of the subtle realm, and the spiritual rest of the causal realm. As far as the physical realm is concerned, everyone knows that after a full day's work one must get rest during the night. After exertion during the day one must stop to rest and gain energy to start again. Everyone knows this, although not everyone knows the art of physical rest.

Rest at the subtle or mental level appears between the fulfilment of one desire and the start of the next desire. This is the state of non-desire which provides rest of the subtle level. One stops all hankerings, and the thinking process comes to stillness.

Rest at the spiritual or causal level is available when all activities of the physical and subtle body—the desires, the thinking process and even the feelings and emotions—are stilled. The causal level is the ultimate initiator of all activity, and when complete satisfaction with everything and every situation is achieved and there is no hankering after any further need, then one gets the rest of the spiritual realm. In that rest the Atman appears, as the sole witness, in its luminous glory and observes the great stillness of the whole universe as one single unit where there is no play of physical movement, mental movement, or even emotional movement. This could be described as 'complete surrender', or 'complete faith in the will of the Absolute'. One simply accepts everything without any rejection or opposition.

Rest at the physical level provides enough energy for eight or nine hours of activity for any individual. This is how the human race keeps going without much trouble. At least people with common sense appreciate this and provide themselves with physical rest, and keep in good health and normal activity.

Rest at the subtle or mental level, by cessation of conflicting desires, brings another dimension to the idea of rest. In this dimension of rest efficiency arises, and this works through all activities—ordinary physical work or artistic work. Thus, rest at this level, between fulfilment of one desire and initiation of another, will be rewarded with efficiency.

The causal or spiritual level of rest, which is profound stillness or total immobility, is in the realm of the

Absolute. Since the causal realm cannot be described, one learns about it from its effects. One can see it in the activities and dispositions of those who provide themselves with spiritual rest. There are three prominent features.

First, they show love and affection towards everything they encounter. All activities are initiated with love, and then held and nourished with love till they come to their fulfilment. All relationships with individuals or activities, direct or indirect, are illuminated and guided only by love and affection.

Second, their ideas, intentions or motives are pure and simple. Purity and simplicity widen the horizon, and they think and work for the whole of humanity and only through the laws of the Absolute. The divisions of groups, races or nations disappear and only natural laws are employed. Their thoughts naturally encompass the whole of the human family, and its intrinsic goodness.

Third, the physical movements of such people are tuned to the natural rhythm, and the result is simplicity and economy of movement. They never rush into any situation, are never agitated, and perform all actions in an efficient, sublime and refined way. Whatever they do will emerge from stillness, be held in stillness, and again submerge in the same stillness which they experience in this great total immobility. This is an ideal or a standard for the common man to aspire to, if he somehow awakes to the need to improve his state.

☆

5 Resonance

The holy scriptures lay down that at all times—in the beginning, in the middle and in the end, all through the past, the present and the future—one should always think of Param-Atman because we do not know when the end may come. But we cannot do this without forming a habit. However, it is wrong to imagine, as some people do, that they will be able to form this habit in their old age. If we do not cultivate this habit in our younger days, it is difficult to do so when we are old. But if you only manage to remember Param-Atman in old age, though not when you were young, He would be satisfied even then!

This world wants your body. Well, serve the world with your body. But Param-Atman wants your love only. If you love Param-Atman, it would be Param-Atman who would then begin to serve you. The Bhagavad-Gita says:

'Through the inner ear of a devotee I make my way into his soul and sweep it clean.'

There are troubles on every path. The path of devotion also has its own troubles, but these troubles carry us forward and form the basis of fresh inspiration. By bearing these troubles the devotion is strengthened. We form the habit of constantly remembering Param-Atman, and are thus able to remember Param-Atman at the time of death. A devotee is desireless, peaceful. He has no enmity. His vision is uniform. He sees Param-Atman in everything.

☆

On the road there are street lights some distance apart.
Each light shines out a certain distance. The lights meet
and the darkness in between disappears. So if you
remember the Lord before going to sleep and remember
Him again when you awake, then the darkness in
between will also be converted into light and it will be
counted as part of your prayer, your remembering.*

☆

All our desires and volitions come as obstacles in our
experiences in meditation, and attention is lost. It is
advisable to have fewer desires. As these desires
decrease attention soon begins to develop. For example,
when water in a pond is agitated, then the reflection of
the sun also moves in broken form, although the sun is
itself not moving. As the movement in the water slows
down, so does the movement of the reflection. Once the
water is completely still, one can see the reflection full
and still. When our mind is stilled, only then can
attention prevail.

☆

Q. How can one remember the guidance throughout
the day?

H.H. During the working day one is involved in Rajas
because one has to keep on being active, and it is in the
nature of Rajas that one all too easily forgets one's
longing for this guidance. It is a natural phenomenon.
But, if it is natural to forget, it is also natural to
remember; so when one recognises that one has
forgotten, one should remind oneself and try to bring

*See page 93

this forgetful state between two moments of remembrance.

If the darkness, which symbolises forgetfulness, is contained between two lights, then it is very easy to cross the darkness without any help from outside, because there is light behind and light in front.

So remembrance reflects some light in the darkness, and one can hold on to the light that lies ahead and go through the darkness.

If there are two remembrances, then one will find that the forgetfulness in between them has lost its force and whatever guiding light the individual needs will become available by remembering again.

The mongoose is a small animal whose nature is to fight snakes. Whenever they meet they fight, and if the snake gives the mongoose a poisonous bite, the mongoose runs away and goes to smell a certain herb. This particular herb nullifies the poison and the mongoose recovers. He returns to the fight again and this process continues as long as the fight goes on. The mongoose withdraws to smell the herb and comes back recharged for the fight, having been cured of the effect of the poison.

To be able to acquire universal grace constantly all one needs to do is to keep one's inner door open, open in the direction of the Absolute. The universal grace of the Absolute permeates the universe so it is available all the time.

If the memory of this universal grace is kept alive, then it forms a connection and allows one to be receptive to grace all the time. Even if it is not constant and the individual's memory is awakened after a little interval, whatever has been done during this period of forgetfulness will be washed out, cleared, burned out so one remains within the realm and influence of the universal grace. Keeping one's door open towards the Absolute, and holding the memory that one is receiving the universal grace are sufficient. Whether the memory is constant or intermittent determines how much grace is received.

Q. His Holiness told us that the Absolute is available everywhere. His love is always available and all one has to do is surrender. Why is it so difficult to surrender when one wants to so much?

H.H. The reason is attachment to the world. Take the example of the sun and the clouds. The sun is always there but the clouds come over and cover the sun and we are unable to see it, although the sun is still present. The world and our attachment to it, these are the reasons, this is our chief hindrance to realising the Absolute. The method to overcome this is prayer, meditation, and things like that. When we are able to reduce this hindrance by these means, then we get some sort of union with the Absolute and there is joy.

We cannot have two priorities at the same time. Either give priority to the world or give priority to the Absolute. As soon as the priority to the world is given up, the Absolute is there. Take the example of a balance. When the two pans are empty then the level is perfectly horizontal. As soon as something is put in on one side, it comes down and the other side goes up. Similarly when the mind is not relieved of these worldly desires, then that side of the balance weighs down.

So to experience the joy, it is necessary to free the mind. Free the balance from all the weight of worldly things.

Q. Remembering or thinking about Param-Atman as the tremendous source of the universe remains for me a cold, intellectual pursuit. It is easier to remember Param-Atman and oneSelf (Atman) together; then a warmth and a sense of unity comes in.

H.H. Remembering or thinking about the Param-Atman as the tremendous source of the universe may possibly appear a somewhat cold, intellectual pursuit. It would not be so, if it were the other way round. Instead of trying to make your thoughts dwell on Param-Atman, let Param-Atman dwell in your thoughts. Then coldness will disappear and warmth will come.

The method to find unity with the universal Param-Atman is to be searching for the truth in your thoughts.

There are two aspects of the creative activity of the Absolute—one which manifests itself and the other which withdraws itself. The creative act of manifestation is rightly performed only if the artist is healthy (one who stays with the Self); healthy in the sense that he is empty, he is not attached and everything about him is pure. Then he looks at, and into, this wonderful creation, elicits all the information and puts everything together in such a way that it makes a good work of art.

Reverse this creative process and you have meditation; in meditation all that we have collected is gradually eliminated and we go deeper and deeper to where there is nothing except the creative force, the Self. One is the art of manifestation, the artistic work; the other is the art of going deep into the Self, which is meditation. These are the two aspects of the creativity of the Absolute.

Here is an example.

Two artists went to a king to make money by exhibiting their art. They told the king that they could create identical works, if the king would like to put them to the test. The king asked 'Are you going to copy each other?' They replied that they would not copy each other at all. They asked if they could each have one end of the hall with a partition built down the middle, so they could live and work separately and promised there would be no difference between their work when the king came to see it. The king did as they asked and they worked for a month. One painted and the other simply polished the wall. At the appointed time, the partition was taken away and, when the light fell upon the painting, it was reflected exactly on the other wall.

The two aspects of the creative act are shown in this story; one is meditation which is polishing, bringing in the brilliance of the Absolute by elimination, so it can reflect everything purely and accurately without distortion. The other is the art which we have to learn in the physical world.

☆

If we want to make a journey we have to find the route on a map or ask directions from people who know the way. But for each individual the direction of this way is not going anywhere else, but going into himself. The trouble is that although we live in our own house, yet we don't know it, we don't remember it. But when we remember the names of the great men who are one with the Atman, then their power guides us round inside our own house. By remembering them we remember ourselves. And so this is a help to us to go to our own Selves.

Q. The hand symbol you showed us (index finger folded against thumb) helps me very much. It reminds me without words of what I am trying to do.

H.H. The sign you mention is known as Jnana Mudra (Knowledge symbol). In this symbol the index finger bows down to meet the thumb. Here the index finger represents the individual ego bowing down to meet the Param-Atman, and the other three fingers symbolise his nature bound by the Law of Three, which is found everywhere. The individual must rise above the law of the three Gunas by continuously being in union with the Absolute to enjoy the full knowledge of the Absolute. As he develops through this experience, many layers of finer and finer knowledge will in due course become clear to him.

The index finger stands for the individual ego. In this finger is plenty of Rajas. If one points this finger at a tender shoot of pumpkin it will dry out and die. This finger is always used for discipline, orders, dictates, reprimands and threats. This is a hard and most rajasic finger! It needs to be united to the truth or the Absolute.

This is what was said by the first Shankaracharya: 'Brahman is the truth and the world is not truth and there is no difference between the individual and Brahman'.

☆

6 The Present Moment

Time is part of the material world. Where there is space, there is time. A long journey takes much time, a short journey less, but in the spiritual world time and space have no validity. One can't think of time in relation to Self-realization. The Self which is to be realized is here, there and everywhere. No one has to journey to find it. It is found only in oneself.

There are different categories of time. One day we think we have very little time, but actually there is enough. Another day we think we have plenty of time, but really it is terribly short. Time mostly relates to the situation. In sleep we see a lot, we cover large areas of time; but as a matter of fact our dreams occupy very little of our time—a dream which covers a big area of time takes very little time to pass through our consciousness. Time is different again in deep sleep; and of course in bliss as well, time has a different measure, so time varies according to the measure.

Here is an illustration. Lakshman, the brother of Rama, told him that he would like to see the great illusion of Maya—the Maya which Rama was always talking about. Rama replied, 'You will get into trouble through seeing it, so I shouldn't bother about it.' Lakshman replied, 'I'm quite sure it won't affect me, and I'm still curious to see it'. So Rama said, 'All right, you'll see it by and by', and left the question open. They went to the river to bathe. When they had finished bathing and both were coming ashore, Rama said, 'My brother, I've lost my ring. Do you think you could dive for it?' He went and dived for the ring; at that moment he lost his consciousness. When he came out of the water, he was in a different land; it was a beautiful countryside. He met there a beautiful woman, and they settled down together, established a home and lived like householders.

He begat four sons and when he became an old man he caught malarial fever, developed a cough and eventually died. His sons took him to the river as the custom was to immerse his body in the water, and as the body submerged, at that moment Lakshman again came out of the water, and out of Maya. He went to Rama with tears in his eyes and repentance in his heart, but still didn't remember what had happened. But Rama said to him, 'You wanted to experience Maya— Illusion. Now you have the experience'.

All the differentiation of time and space which we calculate in this world is illusion. In the Atman there is no time, there is no space, it is all One. In our waking consciousness and in sleep we see a distorted effect of all this.

☆

The present moment is the immanent Absolute, and in the present moment He comes in His form in front of everyone and that is the moment for everyone to appreciate the Absolute. The concept of past and future is involved with worldly affairs, so, when one thinks of the past, one is deviating from the Absolute which is present, and one is trying to have certain relationships with worldly things. When one is planning about the future, then one is deviating from the present Absolute.

There is a Sanskrit verse in which it is said, 'The Absolute is here in the present. See, enjoy and communicate with Him, and do not bother your head with the past or the future.' You cannot bring the past to life, you cannot tailor the future as you want because both things are beyond the control of the individual, so we should bother our head least about the past and the future. With the memory of the Absolute we should try to make use of the present with all the glorious things which the Absolute is here to offer in the present moment.

The present is always lit, because it is the presence of the Absolute, and the light of the Absolute falls on the present. There is nothing to worry about or fear in the present. Past and future are very dark, and that is where the fears are, and it is only fears of some sort which drag individuals to the past or the future. It is much better and more economical for us to avail ourselves of the brilliance and the light and knowledge which are of the present, and not to associate ourselves with the darkness which really belongs to the past or the future. They visit us, and concern us sometimes. Whenever we wake up and find that we are travelling towards the darkness of the past or future, please come into the light of the day—the light of the present.

☆

It has been observed in the scriptures that the wise man behaves like a child, not that his actions are childish but because of his wisdom he is alive to the present; the goodness in a child's action is that whatever the child does it leaves no scar. The child always starts afresh. It may be happy now and may cry next but all in the moment. It enjoys it all and does not hang on to any action. No sooner is the act over, the memory of it is also gone, the happiness or sorrow is gone as if it did not exist. The child is neither bothered by the past nor does it hanker for the future. The wise man who behaves like a child is always filled with bliss. When he has to tackle a situation, he does not leave his bliss; he is not influenced by the deeds of the past or by expectations of the future. He is always in bliss and free.

Q. It seems strange, when it is only our physical body that is limited to seventy or eighty years, that we have such a small limited sense of time. Is it because we don't understand the importance of the present moment, and do not live enough in the moment?

H.H. The concept of time differs from coarse to subtle level. Our lifetime of seventy or eighty years is based on the calculation of the physical world. The physical world has its own pace and all time is related to movement created by nature. The physical body is tuned to that time-scale and so naturally one has to respect that time-scale for all physical activities. One has to be in the present moment to use and enjoy the physical world according to its pace. The concept of time changes when you come to the subtle world.

Meditation mainly concerns the subtle body which is governed by a different time-scale.

If one wanted to go to Badrinath which is 12,000 feet up in the Himalayas, one would need at least fifteen days to cover the journey there and back, some money, clothes, companions in case one got lost, and good health. This one can do on the physical plane, but once you have completed this journey by physical body you can journey there and back in a matter of moments by your subtle body. In this journey you do not need time, money or companions and not even good health. This subtle world reduces this time to a different dimension. Meditation is more of a coming home which is very easy. What one really needs is faith, sincerity and continuous effort. If one meditates faithfully and sincerely and keeps up continuous effort, one would be able to comprehend and complete the journey to the real Self quite soon. A full effort of this sort could bring about growth of being to full freedom in only one year. But in our case it takes much longer, and the length of time seems long or, in other words, the life span seems short to achieve liberation. This is completely wrong. Half an hour twice a day is, in fact, enough, even though we may only use a few minutes of this time. This is enough for the twenty-four hours.

☆

7 Energy and Rest

The creation is full of the three Gunas. Everything is evolved out of these three Gunas and nobody can escape them. What we can escape is the clamouring for them and once we have escaped clamouring for any of the Gunas things should be easy; but it would be impossible to hold on to one of them and leave the others. Every man, every action and every thing is full of the three Gunas; no one can escape them and we have to work with them.

Attachment of any kind is bound to bring misery and bondage, so avoid attachment, even to Sattva.

To meditate is to be in Sattva, but after meditation when you take up any activity, you come into Rajas; when you go to sleep you have to come under Tamas. To be in the world, to live in this creation, one has to use Sattva for a certain period, Rajas and Tamas for certain periods. One should not think that because Sattva is better one should have it all the time. That would be impossible and against nature. If one sees that Sattva is good, one should attempt meditation with more feeling and attention compared with other activities.

The creation is full of this trinity of Sattva, Rajas and Tamas. This is the primal factor. The same three forces are repeated all through the creation to its grossest form. For example, knowledge, change and ignorance; creation, existence and dissolution; in grammar: first, second and third person, or masculine, feminine and neuter gender, and so on. The pattern of three repeats right through creation from the first impulse to the very end. A discriminating man should be able to see more of it in every created form. But one thing must be kept in mind that, although these three forces are working through the creation, there is another factor which only observes the coming and going of three forces reacting on each other.

The need for rest for body, mind and spirit arises only when some activity has been undertaken. Without activity one would not need rest because one would not have spent any energy.

The process of our creation is such that, in the pattern of this universe, both physical activity and physical rest are available. During the day you have activity, and then you retire to get rest at night. The same applies to the mind and spirit—all these assets are provided by nature, and it is necessary for us all to make use of them. We cannot, and we should not put all of them to rest all the time. We must use them and use them fully, so that we can go back to the rest and get all the energy recharged from the centre, and come back again to make use of all these glorious aspects of our nature.

One goes to the river which is flowing all the time full of water, and puts an earthen pot into it. When you submerge the earthen pot in the river, then the water without and within is the same, there is no difference of any sort. The only barrier is the earthen pot itself, but it holds the water which can be used outside the river.

The stream of energy going through the universe all the time is held by the individual like the earthen pot. You take the energy from this stream, use it in your daily affairs, and it should be used up. When it is exhausted, you go back to the stream to be refilled.

The same energy system is available to all of us. The ordinary man uses up his energy every day but only knows how to replenish his physical energy; from physical rest he also gets some mental and spiritual rest, but very little.

So he keeps on going, but he does not really get the best out of his life because he does not get any adequate rest for either the mind or the spirit.

In a diamond mine, thousands of tons of stone are cut 300 feet below ground. It is brought up, broken up into small pieces, processed, washed and then spread out to dry. Thousands of people are engaged in picking over these small stones and looking at them. All this process goes on and ultimately they may find about 100 grammes of diamonds.

This also happens in meditation—so you will have to give half an hour simply to get just a few moments of contact with the Self, and it is worth while because you do get a diamond—the real force, the most valuable precious material of anybody's life.

Or it is like diving to the bottom of the ocean. You bring things to the surface—they are not all precious. You examine what you have brought up, throw away the unnecessary things, and keep and collect anything valuable. It's just like this—going into the ocean, not knowing what you are going to get. You may get many things but out of them you keep the best. Even if only a few minutes of going deep are available it is good, but there is no rule limiting it.

☆

Q. It seems obvious that there is a world of consciousness as well as a world of movement. One wonders why it takes so long to discover it when it is so obvious that in that world of consciousness there is stillness and one cannot be moved.

H.H. Birds have two wings by nature and it is the interplay of both the wings which allows them to fly high in the sky. If one of the wings is cut off or put out of action, then the bird is forced to stay on the earth and it cannot fly any more. Similarly, there are two wings of our existence—the material and the spiritual. Somehow, people seem to prefer the use of one wing only and either cling on to the material wing or the spiritual wing. Since both are naturally necessary, there is much strife in search of bliss. Unless people do realise the need to use both wings and refrain from being partial, they will be deprived of the freedom and bliss which all seek. Unless this truth is realised, the work cannot pick up speed nor can the flight into the spiritual world materialise.

When one goes into meditation one reaches to the source of energy and one gathers back whatever one has spent during the day, or during the year. It only depends upon the purity or quality of meditation as to how much extra energy one will have regained, either to replenish or to refill the lost energy, or get something extra to be able to do more and better work.

The natural law is seen to be regulated by the three Gunas—Sattva, Rajas and Tamas. Two of the three use energy—Rajas and Tamas are there to use up the energy enshrined in the individual. It is only in Sattva that the energy can be recovered and stored up by the individual. The qualities of these three are seen in different manifestations: Sattva is a very light Guna, in two senses. It gives light to the individual and it makes his heart very light—it always keeps him in a happy, steady, evolving, blissful situation. Rajas activates the individual, but the movement is too fast and he doesn't come to any peaceful and steady situation. Tamas brings sloth and laziness and binds everything together, so with Rajas and Tamas the energies of nature are being dissipated and spent. We have been given this meditation to go deep and bring out that energy which can be used again. If the expenses of the individual are more than the income then the downfall is obvious, but, if the income of the individual is more than the expenses, then development is assured. All we have to do is to practise more, so that we get charged with more energy and the rest will follow naturally—things will get done, we will be much happier, much steadier and much more pleasant and effective wherever we are.

☆

It is as if we lived in a house built of bricks and one could not see into all the rooms. It is consciousness which gives one the understanding of the unity of the building. If the whole place were built of glass, one could see all the other rooms and see anybody anywhere. Expansion means being conscious that the universe is a big replica of our own body. There are three types of building where Sattva is like glass, Rajas brick and Tamas steel. All bodies are in fact built of glass; the Rajas of life, however, accumulates dirt so that one can only see out here and there. There is not even a glimpse when the steel of Tamas encases the body. A clear glass makes it possible to see the unity. This means the expansion of consciousness.

Again it can be looked at in this way: a human being has three compartments. The first is Sattvic where peace and light prevail. The Sattvic person is centered here though he uses all three rooms. He moves into the second room for his daily work, but he is still conscious of the light. He uses the lowest room of Tamas for sleep. Here there is no light, but whenever he gets up he moves into the other rooms. The man of Rajas is centered in the second room. He has no knowledge of the first room but he has some ideas about it. The man of Tamas lives entirely in the third room, and for him the other two do not exist. They are neither cleaned nor looked after, and eventually fall into decay. It is important for us to use all three.

You get rest during sleep but in that rest Tamas predominates. Meditation is the rest of Sattva. Full rest is when vibrations stop; that is real meditation.

Usually, during meditation, something external comes into your world. For example—if you have a full night's sleep, say six hours, you are refreshed. Nothing from outside has come into your body; but if you get four hours, or even two hours, instead of a full night's sleep, then to some extent you feel refreshed but not fully.

This rest which you get in meditation is Sattvic due to release of Sattva. So even a half-hour's meditation makes you entirely fresh.

I must remind you that during meditation no energy from outside comes into our body, the energy is already in the body.

How then do we get rest? Because those energies, vibrations and agitations subside and their subsidence makes you feel fresh.

The object of meditation is to give you energy for all your actions—worldly and non-worldly; for these you need energy; so, as you meditate, that energy goes on accumulating. We also expend energy during our daily work.

Here is an example. If you have a bank account, then you get a certain interest on it. The energy you get from meditation is that remaining in the body, but out of this energy there is also interest, as with a bank account. You use that interest for carrying out your worldly jobs.

☆

Sattva is light; Rajas activates the individual and is also used for whatever work is presented to us, but one cannot go on with Rajas all the time, so nature will call us to take some rest (Tamas), and this is the cycle.

We collect different types of food and fruit and we cook them to make them ready for our consumption, but together with the food we add a little salt to make the whole thing palatable. Salt, by itself, is not a food but an aid to food. In the same way Sattva itself is not a food as such, it is not for living but just to help living. Through Sattva one gets energy, and if one gets energy one must use it. So one cannot resign from Rajas and Tamas; one has only to learn to love Atman. This love of Atman will keep everything else at a distance and in its place where it will not have too much attraction. This will give one a vision of the Self, and also vision from the Self, which will keep everything in proper proportion.

There are three types of memory. Memory imbued with Tamas is lost immediately; you lose everything that you have observed; the impressions vanish out of the mind. Memory with Rajas is sharp but short-lived and may be distorted. It's always on the move, it's not yours and will go away. The third type of memory arises from Sattva. This is the memory that people hold even in dreams. Most dreams are in Tamas and we don't remember them when we wake up; other dreams are associated with Rajas and we remember some of them; but there are certain dreams that we never forget. They are the dreams that come from Sattva.

☆

8 Desires

Dr. R. I would like to re-tell a story.

A man had two sons. The younger asked for his portion of the inheritance and went to a far country where he 'wasted his substance in riotous living'. Now there came a great famine on the land, and being reduced to the condition of a swineherd he would even desire to eat the pig's food; but when 'he came to himSelf' he said, 'How many hired servants of my father have food enough and to spare, and yet I perish with hunger. I will arise and go to my father'. When he was yet a great way off, his father met him and kissed him, and made the servants put the best robe on him and prepare a feast. But the elder son was working in the fields, and when he was told what was happening, he complained that though he was always faithful, his father never made a feast for him. But the father said, 'Son, you are always with me and all that I have is yours, but this, your brother, was dead and is alive again; he was lost and is found.'

If the father was the Atman, who are the sons, and who receives the 'good impulse'?

H.H. The father is the Atman or the Absolute. The sons are men, one with understanding and one with ignorance. The son without understanding associates himself with body and its claims. So he asks the father to give him his portion. In doing so he only establishes a boundary within the creation which he could call his own. He then goes out into the search of pleasure far removed from the centre of happiness into the realm of the material world. This 'far country' is the country where the physical laws prevail, and when the physical body has spent the substance, there comes a famine due to lack of rest and real bliss. Utterly confused and miserable, and then not being able to see further, he looks back or looks within. He remembers to look within because of the great misery. He remembers the wealth and abundance of his father's house where everyone is happy, and compares his situation with others. He is then met by his father midway and is given the robe. The giving of the robe is the dawn of discrimination of true knowledge, and then all become happy and make a feast. He starts a new life because a transformation has taken place due to discrimination and true knowledge. When the other son asks why he was never given a feast, he is told that the feasts are given to those who have been separated. Those who are united with the Father, they are always celebrating. There is not a moment when there is no happiness in the company of the Father. The outer celebration is only for the separated ones, and since the younger was separated from wisdom he was given a special treatment to start afresh. One who is with the Father is without blemish, and one who is without blemish is indeed the Absolute. In the Absolute there is fullness and completeness, and in fullness there is no blemish.

All living things seem to be crying out for something or other. Among mankind some pray for wealth, some for health, some for property, some for fame, some for power, some for freedom from troubles, some for food and basic necessities during life. Moreover, all want what they ask for to be on a permanent basis; nobody wants merely a temporary cure or temporary riches. Also, we want these things in full measure; and nothing which is less than full is good enough, our object being to make and keep ourselves full in all respects.

When one is a child, one wants toys; when one is a boy, one wants education; when one's education is over, one wants employment; when one gets employment, one wants promotion. Thus, from the beginning to the very end, there is never contentment.

The great Moghul Emperor, Akbar, while out hunting once had to spend the night in the jungle. Unable to sleep owing to the noise made by jackals, he asked why they were crying. Someone said that it was on account of the cold. Akbar ordered blankets to be distributed to the jackals, but still they went on crying. When Akbar again asked the reason, he was told that it was on account of their joy at getting the blankets!

In this way satisfaction in stillness and peace never comes to us, and we always go on crying!

The remedy is devoting yourself to Param-Atman. With this, all the unnecessary thinking of worldly needs comes to an end, and thereafter is succeeded by realization of Param-Atman. Only then is there complete satisfaction; wanting nothing, we feel full. A union takes place between the full Self and the full Param-Atman. These two aspects of fullness mingle inseparably, never to part again.

☆

When people go to the village market from distant places or from mountain tops, they hear the hustle and bustle of the market din which gives them an approximate guide to the whereabouts and direction and distance to the market place which they cannot see. They know that it is there. Having completed the journey, they join in the market affairs and become part of the market din. They forget that they and the din are not the same. Similarly, most men become part of this transitory material world and forget the identity of the detached observer for whose pleasure and benefit the market and the world were initially created.

Every individual has desires, and we are plagued with these desires, but there is some time between each of them. Most of the time we do not allow this interval to stretch at all; no sooner is one desire fulfilled than we let another desire spring up. If people understood this and allowed themselves the luxury of a little interval, however short it might be, they would find that they would re-charge themselves without doing anything but just being quiet for a moment or two. If people could practise this and enlarge this interval—say up to five minutes at one stretch—they would find that they had great power within, and the potentiality of realising themselves would not be far off if they could do this, giving themselves the luxury of two minutes of interval between one desire and the rising of the next.

☆

The canal

The fewer and steadier our desires, the more the power, and the facility to fulfill them.

Take the example of a canal—when it is constructed to irrigate the fields, hundreds of small openings are made into the canal to allow the water into the fields. But if you have hundreds of openings, then the amount of water being put into the fields will be less than if you have only ten openings.

The application of meditation is just one such way to curtail our desires, because you give some time to it, and it takes you away from your lovely desires. The extension of this moment of peace between two desires is another way. Understand this central point: that consciousness is only consumed through desires—the fewer the desires, the better use of consciousness that can be made. All the disciplines which we have been given are to lead in this direction—if we practise extending the moment of peace between two desires, we can get the full benefit of this process.

The drama of Maya is a universal act and this has to go on in eternity. It will never stop. So obstacles and confusion will always be there. As long as you don't have any playful association with them, if you are not interested in them, you can avoid them, just as a moment ago you avoided the mobile loudspeaker which went down the road. So it is good to avoid them simply and sincerely. The main or violent obstacles must be handled properly, for they can be very explosive. So extra effort should be made to avoid them. But the ordinary obstacles and confusions are a part of the creation and our lives; we cannot undo them and if someone really wanted a quiet place, devoid of any distractions, it would be hard to find one. The remedy is just to ignore the lot and pick up what is important. One has to use discrimination.

There was a king who went out on a horse and after some time both he and his horse became very thirsty. In his search for water, he came across a well from which water was being pumped by mechanical means. This made a lot of noise and his horse wouldn't drink because it was nervous and distracted by the noise. So the king asked the workmen to stop it for a little while so his horse could drink. But when they stopped the pump, of course, there was no water available. He tried two or three times, and then the foreman said 'Dear King, if you can make your horse drink this water in spite of this noise, well and good; otherwise look for somewhere to sleep instead!'

The moral is that our mind is like the horse. Although it is interested in drinking the water of spiritual knowledge, it is so lost in the distraction of the outward noise that it cannot drink. Wise men, however, while aware of these noises, ignore them, and only pay attention to what is useful to the Atman.

☆

Dr. R. There is a story about a tramp who slept in Hyde Park and was happy because he always dreamt he was sleeping in the Ritz Hotel. Someone who was interested in him booked him a room for the night in the Ritz. Next morning they asked him how he had slept. 'Very badly', he replied, 'I spent the night dreaming I was sleeping on a hard bench in the Park!'

H.H. The story is very useful in understanding the working of the human mind. It is never satisfied with what it has, and always desires something quite different. While a poor man envies the comforts of the rich and wants to be rich too, a rich man is weary of his anxieties and envies the carefree sleep of one who has nothing. A sick man worries about getting well, only making his sickness worse, while a man in good health worries that he may get ill.

The mind also has a tendency to live more in the past and the future, and less in the present which is much more important than either. This combination of dissatisfaction with the present and the perpetual desire for something different in the future causes perpetual unhappiness. The remedy is to see, with the eye of true knowledge, the same thing in everything, and that same thing is Param-Atman. Then the outlook becomes balanced and unified, unrest giving place to tranquillity.

In our day-to-day actions (on the physical level), however, as apart from our thoughts, things should be taken as they are, and not everything as the same.

Dr. R. It has been found that mind is either running into past or future and not making use of the present moment for Self-realization.

H.H. There was a lawyer; he got married and after some time he and his wife started planning their future. The lawyer suggested that when they had a son, they should bring him up and educate him to become a lawyer, even better than his father. The wife had something else in mind. She wanted her son to become a doctor because her parents were in the medical profession. Arguments started and they became heated. While they were arguing a holy man happened to appear and asked them why they were fighting. The husband explained his ambitions and the wife stated hers. The holy man asked them to call the boy and enquire what he would like to be. The couple said, 'But the child is not yet born!'

One should keep one's mind only on useful work.

A servant went to a holy man and offered his services. The holy man asked what remuneration he required. The servant said that he would take only what he needed to eat, but there would be one condition, 'I must always be provided with work and in the absence of work I will destroy you.' The holy man agreed. In a day or two the hermitage was completely organized and routine work regulated, and the servant was without work. He asked for further work and restated the condition. The holy man asked him to go to a jungle and fetch a tall, strong bamboo pole. He readily did so. Then he was asked to fix it firmly in the ground and keep climbing up and down unless he was called for some other work. He must continue to do all the little things for him but in all his spare time he must climb up and down without a rest. The servant got tired very soon and came with an apology and asked to be forgiven for his disrespect and withdrew his condition.*

It is the same with the mind. Its nature is to remain active. It always wants some work. So keep it busy in useful work. One can at most do ten hours of work and take six hours of sleep. The rest of the time (eight hours)

*See page 54

the mind should be given useful work,—in meditation, good company, study of good literature or scriptures. Make your mind work for the Master and don't allow it to establish a kingdom of its own to do whatever it wants.

Everyone is free but thinks that they are bound. In fact all those things that bind them are the expression of their own ignorance. This is what everyone has to understand. Here is an example. A special trick is used to catch monkeys. A round earthen pot with a small mouth is buried in the ground. Pieces of tasty food are put inside. When the monkeys smell them, they come close and put their hands inside and clutch the food, and then they cannot pull them out. The monkey doesn't know that he can be free. He doesn't want to release the piece of food, and yet wants to be free, so he cries, and can't run away. At that moment the man appears from his hiding place and catches the monkey. Most people who think that they are not free are acting like the monkey. They are holding on to something, maybe things of beauty, or fragrance. If only they could release their hold, they would be free, because in truth they are free.

True knowledge is made available to everyone, to show that all this beauty is really the creation of your own Self. It is free to be enjoyed and to give the bliss which is what you really want. Don't attach yourself to anything because, the moment you do so, the bliss will disappear. This creation is totally free; there is no bondage whatsoever. You can appreciate everything in this creation and be happy. You need not be attached and miserable, trying to be free. You are free and you are made free and a free man knows that everyone is free.

After all, what is misery? Give someone one suit of clothing or a hundred, will they be satisfied? Will they not hanker for different or better ones? Happiness and misery are not caused by lack of food or clothing. They are both a product of the mind. As long as one allows oneself to be identified or mentally caught up, one can be miserable without food or with plenty of food. Who really knows that the poor, the weak or the unsheltered are living in misery? Equally, who knows that the rich are happy? As often as not they lack the zest to enjoy things they buy, or can't digest their food, or lack health to enjoy natural surroundings. One should not judge the condition of the Atman by poverty or sickness. One should look always to the cause—what brings misery? It may be covered in silk or it may be naked. Nor should one conclude that death is the ultimate answer for the relief of misery. Release from misery comes from true knowledge which takes no account of riches or poverty, sickness or health. Discrimination is the key. Through it one can see one's own desires for things one lacks, and one can also see that those who have the things one covets are not happy. Neither happiness nor misery dwell in things, but in one's own decision, made through discrimination, that acquisition of worldly things will bring neither. Following that decision detachment comes, releasing from misery and bringing happiness.

People have forgotten the real meaning of happiness. People take pleasure in happiness. Pleasure and pain are derived from material things and their association with one's state of mind. Pleasure and pain chase each other like day and night. Man's relation to pleasure and pain is always temporary and always changing and everyone gets his share of these two. True happiness is one of the natural manifestations of the Self. There are three states: Truth, Consciousness and Bliss. The real Self can never exist without these three aspects. This is a higher state of being.

When one limits oneself to a petty desire, then one gets pleasure when the desire is fulfilled and pain when it is not fulfilled.

You go to a theatre and see actors in laughter and tears and because you are only watching and observing the play without being involved in it, you come out happy. So happiness is that which is derived from truth and consciousness. In the case of the play, from the true characterisation and conscious plan you enjoy truth and consciousness. One should be very careful not to confuse happiness with pain and pleasure.

The whole of our mind has for so long been associated with the outer world that it has quite forgotten the existence, let alone the language of the inner world. The moving mind looks for happiness in getting and experiencing things. These do not suffice, for, when the mind has one thing, it immediately rushes after another. The still mind finds happiness in everything.

☆

This kingdom within or the heaven within is the reservoir of peace and bliss. No violence can reach there. Devotion is the gentle art of unity.

In our worldly life we look for pleasure, and we strive hard to snatch those moments of pleasure. Once you get an atom of bliss, you long for more. The craving for pleasure becomes less because of the depth and strength of joy in bliss. For example, you don't care about the well when you get to a lake or river. Bigger and better things reduce the importance of small and inferior things. Dive in with devotion and swim around gently in that blissful heaven which is within you.

Unless one has rest in love and happiness one cannot survive, just as the body cannot survive without sleep. Meditation is to provide rest. To take people to bliss is simply to give them rest—rest with the Self—so that they may have new and fresh mornings of life.

Knowledge of anything is a source of pleasure or pain. Through knowledge we associate ourselves with things or events and then derive pain and pleasure. This is the nature of worldly knowledge. In ignorance there is no pain and no pleasure, no bliss. But behind the structure of knowledge flows the True Knowledge which does not bind us. This is spiritual knowledge. With this we rise above the results of pain and pleasure and enjoy bliss even in the midst of actions.

☆

9 Needs of the Day

The state of profound peace experienced as the Self is like going to have a bathe in the Ganges. When you come out of the river, then you are a bit wet; you do not bring the whole Ganges with you, but you bring the effect of the Ganges and you feel fresh, and you take to any activity in a far better way than if you were tired and unclean.

When you come out of this profound peace, you take something of this great stream of the Ganges with you—the great stream of the Absolute. You acquire some strength from it, and with that strength you deal with all the situations that are presented to you in the world.

☆

Q. Many housewives like me have a day that could be filled many times over with jobs to be done. I enjoy the work and when the remembrance of the Param-Atman comes my heart is warmed instantaneously. Why do I so often let things separate me from the real doer?

H.H. The relationship between the universal and the individual—the Param-Atman and the Atman—that relationship is always present. There is never a moment when this relationship is not working, but we forget it. This happens because we get involved with other things and do not remember the real doer. But the relationship is always there. We should not feel that, even in our ignorance, or by not remembering the Atman, the relationship would be dissolved.

It becomes alive only when the consciousness comes into action, which means when one consciously remembers the Param-Atman. Then it gets activated.

For example, electricity is conducted through wires and contacts, but the energy of the electricity only flows when the switches are turnéd on: so we have to turn on the switches to get united with the energy that is always available.

We know that we forget it. To help this forgetfulness one has somehow to convince one's mind and come to a decision, a decision that will not be altered by any other force later on. A decision such as this—that all our activities are done because of the inspiration of the Absolute and they are done only for the Absolute, and are being done by the forces made available by the Absolute. If one comes to this sort of decision, then one will see that the remembering becomes much more frequent. There may not be constant remembering, but nevertheless it will arise much quicker.

In the street lamp-posts are placed at intervals to illuminate particular places and the light spreads and gradually fades from the source, so that in between the lamp-posts very little light is available. However, there is still enough light to show the way. Two rememberings are like these two lamps; in between there is no remembering, but it is affected by the two rememberings.*

So one should decide in one's mind once and for all that all activities are for the Param-Atman and whenever one has enough consciousness to remember, one should remember; and even if there is no remembering

*See page 60

in between, then at the end of the work one should try to remember again. This will fill every part of your activities with light and consciousness.

☆

Each being is provided with certain assets or talents which he has to make use of for himself, his family, his society, his nation, and so on. Everyone has to understand how much energy is available to him to make use of in a particular place and time.

This relates to the principle that one does not have to think about what one cannot do; one should always keep on thinking about what one can do.

A man had to travel ten miles away to attend to some urgent work. It was late at night and very dark. He took his lantern and came out of the house. He looked out and saw that pitch darkness prevailed the whole ten miles to his destination. He thought of his small lantern and wondered how he could find his way through the darkness. Fortunately, a holy man passed by and he enquired why the man was pausing at the threshold. The man expressed his fear of travelling ten miles with a light which only shone ten feet. The holy man told him not to worry because the moment he stepped forward, the light would also move forward. The light would always be ten feet ahead of him, so he should not worry, just proceed. So he did, and reached his destination.*

Whatever power has been enshrined in the individual should be used in the best possible way. Electricity is provided through the proper wires and connections, but if anyone tries to use a 12 volt bulb to deliver 240

*See page 106

volts it will fuse. This means that individuals, having certain limits to manifest the glory, cannot claim, cannot have any extra power because they are not designed like that; and this, each of us has to realise.

The ant has a particular measure of power and within those limits, it has to perform its activities. The elephant has a different measure of power and accordingly a different body. The ant cannot perform the deeds of the elephant, nor can the elephant perform the deeds of the ant.

When one is busy during the day one can do one thing—before beginning any particular action one should remember the Absolute, and, when this action has been completed, then one should remember the Absolute again. If it is possible some time during the action also to remember, that is well and good. Otherwise, if one could remember the Absolute at the start of a job and at the end of a job, then one is open to the influence of the Absolute during a busy day.

Q. I feel sorry that I get pulled away from Atman. I would like to do things more from my centre.

H.H. If you feel you are removed from the centre, that is the most important thing. This is the strength of Sattva. To be active in the world is no bad thing, for this is your destiny. For example, if someone works hard in the heat of the sun he is doubly appreciative of the shade of the tree. If you are very busy in your ordinary life, go on doing it, but the moment you come back to meditation, the pleasure and peace will be specially deep. All who want to give this peace to others have a special responsibility. They must not withdraw from the active world. If they did, people would think that they are trying to escape from it. That is not what the meditation is for. Be active, exert yourself, exhaust yourself if need be, but keep alive the thread leading to Sattva which calls on you to come back home to meditate and get the energy for next time.

10 Troubles

The ways of Param-Atman are beyond human comprehension. Many things are happening around us, some good and some bad, and we are unable to explain them. We wonder how Param-Atman, who is good, could cause or allow bad things to happen. But 'good' and 'bad' are just comparative notions, and there cannot be anything good unless there is something bad by contrast.

These notions of 'good' and 'bad' constantly create conflicts in our minds and do not allow us any peace. The way to get over all this is to dissociate ourselves from the events viewed, and associate ourselves with the viewer of the events—the Param-Atman.

Param-Atman is the cause of everything and is everything. The world we see is nothing; it was never anything in the past, and will never be anything in the future. Param-Atman is, and is everything; he is the friend as well as the enemy; he is the saint and the householder; he is the beast and the man: he is the sorrow, the attachment and everything else.

Such things worry us as they do in a dream; yet nothing of the dream remains when we wake up. What else could all this be except the most wonderful show?

Q. Why are we born, live in confusion so much of the time, and die in fear and pain, never having understood any of it?

H.H. The design of this universe expressed by the blissful desire of the Absolute is very simple. It is designed to produce bliss all the way through. The whole of this creation is for enjoyment but it is necessary to resort to right ways, right means and right actions. It has never been said that there will be no difficulties in this creation, which is a blissful creation, but the reason for the creation is only knowledge and bliss. Why then should one find confusion, pain and fear, and die without any understanding? In this creation everything exists plain and simple even today, but our education, our social and cultural systems make the simple become complicated; the blissful becomes painful, and what should be love becomes fear. Only through the systematic knowledge which is being given, through the scriptures, and through 'Satsang' (good company), can people be brought back to the simple way of life, and then they will see for themselves that there is no reason for confusion, fear or pain.

As regards the concept of pain—there are people in this world who are adventurous and who take great pleasure in going through all the difficulties and hazards of the adventure, which are sometimes painful. These men never experience the pain—they experience the hardness of what they have to go through, but not pain at all. It arises when one allows oneself, one's body and mind to go through a difficult passage; and yet one does not seem to feel the difficulties because one has taken them on voluntarily. These difficulties then create deeper happiness.

☆

There are difficulties in the way. They mostly come when something good has arrived. Divine forces are always met by difficulties, but once you stick to what is good they turn back. When an elephant passes through the village, the dogs bark and keep barking up to the village boundary. Beyond that they don't go, but turn back. A good or divine knowledge which is new is always met by the barking dogs in our mind. Once you elevate your being, they stop.

Keep upright and try to see yourSelf in everyone. The Self (Atman) lives in everyone, even in those who oppose, so respect even your enemy. Give a proper answer when necessary, and keep your mind free from any malice.

☆

There can be no darkness without light. Do not be afraid of the darkness, there is light beyond it. If there is total darkness, then even a small light will shine out. But when the place is completely illuminated, the small light appears very insignificant, almost negligible. When you feel you are lost in darkness, this creates fear, but do not be afraid, because there is light shining beyond it. Have full faith in it—that there is light and that will remove your fear completely.

Even if you only possess a little light, that is fully capable of taking you to reach your ultimate goal. Do not be afraid that your own power is so little, so negligible. Maybe it is little, maybe it is not illuminating the whole of your path, but, whenever you move forward, it will illuminate the path immediately in front of you and, as you go ahead, it will provide light further ahead. There is no need to lose heart.

Compared with the huge size of the universe we live in, this human body of ours is like a speck of dust. Compared with the unlimited consciousness of the Param-Atman, our mind is like a drop in the ocean. And the problem before us is how to tackle that great consciousness with such limited means—a hopeless business apparently! But hope comes from the saying, 'God helps those who help themselves', which is fortunately true.

The real cause of failures is not the inadequacy of means but an inadequacy of understanding and of determination. Provided we understand what is required, and provided our determination is strong enough, a very little can achieve great results, because on seeing the invincibility of our determination, the heart of Param-Atman melts and He Himself comes to our help.

This is illustrated by the story of the two birds whose eggs were washed away by the sea. They made up their minds to fill up the sea. They picked up drops of sea water in their tiny beaks and dropped them on the beach, and from there they picked up some sand and dropped it in the sea. This went on for some time. Seeing them doing this, other birds also joined them till it became a curious sight to see.

Rishi Agastya happened to pass that way and, on seeing such activity, he enquired what it was all about. The birds told him their story.

'Do you really think,' asked the Rishi, 'that you could complete this work even by labouring all your life night and day?'

'No. But we are determined to devote not only this life but a thousand lives, or even more, to this work till it is completed. We are certainly not going to put up with the injustice that the sea has inflicted on our innocent offspring'.

The Rishi was moved by the just cause of the birds and their strong determination to recover their eggs from the sea. He used his yogic powers to restore the birds' eggs to them.

This is a standard story, always quoted to illustrate how strong your determination should be if you are small and your task great.

What we call 'good' and what we call 'evil'—both exist in the world as necessary antidotes to each other. At times the 'good' becomes proud of itself and therefore ceases to be 'good'; then the 'evil' arises to destroy it. Similarly, when the 'evil' outstrips its functions, it is destroyed by the 'good'. We see examples of this in history (and especially in times like ours when everything is in the melting-pot).

Q. It seems to me that His Holiness is trying to get us to understand that, by dwelling on our short-comings and deficiencies, we are preventing the power of Param-Atman from reaching us?

H.H. Your observation is right—all activities which are initiated by an individual are aimed at some sort of gain, gain not in the bad sense, but personal advancement; but, whenever one thinks about one's previous actions and becomes involved with them, a sort of identity is created between something that has happened and the person who ponders over it. Since a mistake has been made, you are tying yourself to the mistake. All mistakes are taking away precious energy which could equally be used for better actions, so, if you keep on thinking about your mistakes or short-comings in the past, then you are wasting energy.

If you can avoid this waste, then it would be possible for you to engage your attention on the next moment, a process which promises to bring you extra energy by merging with the Absolute or Param-Atman, or any action related to the Param-Atman.

When Krishna was leaving after the war, all others asked for this or that favour. When the turn of Kunti came, she said, 'Give me some adversity or other to remain with me all the time.'

'But why adversity?'

'Because in the past I always thought of You and brought You near me whenever there was adversity, and never when there was none'.

Within each person, there lives the universal Param-Atman, along with the individual Atman for the purpose of guidance. Therefore, we get a guiding voice from time to time when we are in difficulties. In order to hear the inner voice, we should pray to the all-knowing Param-Atman in solitude with a settled mind. Then an answer, to bring us face to face with success, is sure to come forth.

Q. Once or twice I have had a great desire to help someone in difficulty and I have realised that I cannot help, but all I can do is meditate from this desire, and the right help might be given from elsewhere. Can help come in this way?

H.H. There is a much better way of helping others. It is not to have the desire as such but to meditate so purely that there is such a wealth of goodness in the individual that anyone who is in need can come and get it naturally. In this way it will be abundantly available to everyone, very much like the sun which does not direct its light to any single place, but anyone who wants to have help or light from the sun can take it. So the better way is to have finer energy or more Sattva in oneself; this can be used by anybody who needs it.

There are four points to be considered in visualising how to pass the good influence of the Param-Atman to the world. On one side is unity, the Param-Atman, where there is no trouble. On the other side is the world of multiplicity and divisions. Because of these divisions, troubles arise. Between these two extremes, you find certain Realized Men, Holy Men, who have renounced the world and have acquired balance in their lives. They treat everyone as themselves. They treat everyone as Param-Atman. So whatever guides them, they will do their job. Between these Realized Men and the world are groups of people who take advice and guidance from a living Realized Man who can tell you what the Param-Atman is and what you are yourself. There is no division between any individual and the Param-Atman. This message you have to bring into your life. All divisions must go. Unless you dissolve the divisions, you will not be able to pass on the knowledge and the unity. That is the job. These are the four points.

Those who are the victims of injustice, those who have not, those who are deprived of a job, of a good position, housing—all sorts of difficulties exist in their lives. There are also people who have enough. They have wealth, property etc., but even the people who have more than they need are not necessarily really happy. They don't live in bliss. They themselves are in trouble. Their troubles are different. People of the first kind are troubled by one thing, the people of the second kind are troubled by another, but in fact both are in trouble. This is the life of the world of multiplicity. Because there is no unity, troubles of different types arise.

☆

Q. Sometimes, when standing on a mountain top and experiencing the full beauty of creation, the mind quietens and power seems to flow from the universal to the individual, then an intense longing arises in the heart for complete union. Could H.H. say what it is that stops these moments developing to completion?

H.H. There are occasions, as you have described, when there is an abundance of Sattva. There then arises a moment when one experiences the beauty of creation. One feels at one with the universe. It is natural that a desire should arise to maintain this unity with the universe, for as long as possible. One then finds there are difficulties. The difficulties occur only because we slip away from the state of Sattva to Rajas and Tamas. If we are in Rajas, then everything will happen according to Rajas, or if in Tamas, according to Tamas. This is the only difficulty. If we can maintain our state with Sattva there should be no difficulty.

Q. Does this mean that these states could be prolonged indefinitely if one had enough Sattva?

H.H. You should do exactly what you have been doing—go to the mountain-top again!

☆

11 Confidence

Any effort made on the way is itself a realization of the way. Slowly and steadily everything is being done, and one doesn't have to worry about the end of the journey which is where there would be nothing further to do at all. All one can do is to make these little efforts from day to day. Making the effort is itself a part of the realization of the work, and one feels happy that these efforts are being made towards understanding the words.

A certain man had to go out to another town miles away. It was night and pitch dark, and all he had was a tiny little lantern which could, at most, light a couple of steps. Because the journey seemed so long, and the night dark, he was depressed and unsure—unsure of reaching his destination with only this tiny light.

While he stood at his door utterly frustrated and helpless, a Realized Man happened to appear and asked him why he was standing at his door with a lantern.

The man replied that he really did not know what to do; though he was all set for the journey, it appeared so long, and the night so dark, that his small lantern could not really be of much use.

The Realized Man explained to him that it was not necessary to have a light big enough to illuminate the whole way. 'As you proceed' he said, 'the light will move with you, so that the next one or two steps will always be clear. All you need do is to hold on to this light and start walking. As the darkness clears with the rising of the sun, if you keep walking you will reach the destination in the full light of noon'.*

*See page 94

The same applies to one's little efforts. After hearing the words, however small the efforts one can make, the light will be enough for the goal to be achieved. Then there wi'l be nothing else to do except enjoy the full bliss of union.

☆

Q. How to improve the quality of my attention, by better concentration in meditation, as I feel this would be a way to increase my capacity of love for the Param-Atman?

H.H. Although individuals do feel a separate identity, in reality there is only one identity, and that is the Param-Atman. Within us we have this individuality but because of ignorance and other influences it seems to feel separate from the Param-Atman, and that is why it wants to unite with the Param-Atman. For this unity of the individual and the universal it seems as if the effort is being made by the individual himself. The individual, if indeed he does anything at all, only removes the impediments which block his vision of unity with the Param-Atman. In fact, the movement is only from the Param-Atman's side. It is Param-Atman Himself who reaches out to the individual. The love or devotion should be developed by removing the impediments and that, of course, is possible through the meditation and the attention which one brings into one's life; and this, in a way, removes the separate identity of the individual which is composed of his name, his form and his nature. All these things have got to be given up for the real unity or for the real love towards the Param-Atman. The effort is, of course, made by the individual, but he

makes little effort. The greater effort is made by the
Param-Atman. A small child has small legs, so he can
take only small steps, but a big man can walk faster and
cover more ground. The same applies to the individual,
who is a very small being, and to the Param-Atman
which has no limit. This is how the unity of the
individual and the Param-Atman should be made.

All individuals are the Absolute themselves, and so
are you. It is only a question of realizing that one is the
Absolute. To realize that, one has to do away with those
impediments, and to illustrate this here is a story about
a lion cub.

Once, in the forest, a lioness who had several cubs
went off to search for food and while she was away, one
of the cubs strayed into the middle of a flock of sheep.
The cub followed the sheep and the shepherd, seeing
the cub with the sheep, kept him. The cub behaved like
the sheep because of the company of the sheep. The
shepherd thought that, if he remained in this forest,
then one day the lioness would roar and the cub,
hearing the roar, would remember it was a lion and
would attack the sheep. So he took the flock with the
cub to another forest where he believed there were no
lions.

One day a lion did roar in this other forest and all the
sheep ran away, and the cub also tried to run away. The
lion—in lion language!—told the cub to stop and said,
'Why are you afraid of me? There is no need; you are not
a sheep. You are a lion like me. If you are not sure I can
show you'. So he took him to a pond and the little lion
saw in the reflection that he had the same face and same
characteristics as the one who roared. Then the lion
asked him to roar with him, so he learnt how to roar,

and the whole personality and individuality of this little lion was completely changed and he started roaring like a grown lion.

All our efforts in the world are learning the language of the world, which is like the language of sheep and the life of sheep. By good company, the company of saints, and through the discourses, we learn to give up the language of the world and take to the language of the spirit. Once we have learnt and have seen how saintly persons who are much nearer the Absolute conduct their lives, we can also be like this young lion and start behaving like a proper lion, because we are all proper lions by nature.

Knowledge is unlimited and available at all times. It manifests itself according to the need of the time. It is only available when the need arises. The stream of love and truth is one, but man catches it in two different ways, by heart or by mind. By heart he means his love, by mind he means his knowledge. But in fact the stream of love and truth is always the same. It is always present in the world and always will be present in the world but people will only take as much as their destiny offers, or as they need.

Knowledge is not bound to any land or place. No place is favoured. Knowledge is everywhere, all over. If certain types of people are prepared at a place, they will receive it. Preparation of mind is the only key to where this knowledge will descend. If people at a particular place take to the ordinary way of life, they will get ordinary knowledge. If at a certain place people are preparing themselves for higher knowledge, certainly it will be available. No place is particular for knowledge.

Anywhere, anytime, anybody who is looking for this knowledge must get it, because the Absolute is not for a single race, colour, creed or nation.

The macrocosm and the microcosm are both created of the same elements; what is in the universe is in us too. Let the mind go. Release tension and try to think within. This is fundamental; unless you expand, you remain limited. One should remember that one is far bigger than one thinks. If one remembers that one embraces everything, one can draw strength and power from everything. Fear nothing, for nothing is bigger than you.

One should never be nervous about being asked to tackle anything. One has all the power necessary to achieve everything within oneself. It is only necessary to remember the power. If people are nervous, it is because they forget their potentialities and remember only their limitations.

There is no time-limit for Self-realization. It could happen quickly in minutes, or take as long as one could take. Once the mind is stilled and impurities cleared, then one is near the goal. The time-factor depends on the level of being.

The guide is always with the disciple. There is no question of leaving him at all. The guide will never leave him unless he sees the disciple reach his goal of Self-realization. Even death would not break the relationship, so one should be carefree because the help from the guide is assured. As long as realization hasn't been achieved by the disciple, a mental picture remains in the mind of the Self-realized man until the disciple has reached his goal and they are united. One can be very sure of being cared for.

As much as one draws inner strength from meditation, so inner impulses will reach one in time of need. One should have no worry, just faith that in need help will be available according to the need. In deep meditation all are connected by love and affection. This love and affection demands nothing and has neither reason nor motive, it just *is*. Have trust and your need will be fulfilled. As you progress, your influence will become more positive. Keep working.

When the rains come the pots which have their mouths towards the sky get filled with water, but if they face the earth they would not get even a drop of water. In the same way grace is raining from the Absolute, True Knowledge and the Teacher. From the Absolute the rain of grace is eternal and also from the knowledge, but a teacher appears in a certain age and all those who have faith receive the grace of the teacher.

☆

The little Sattva you have got is much more important for you than all the drawbacks, difficulties and troubles you see in the world.

Iron is a cheap metal and gold is a precious metal. There may be a lot of iron lying about but a little gold is worth more than all the iron; that little piece of gold, say an ornament, you keep in a beautiful case; you don't worry about the iron at all.

The little Sattva that you possess is already more than all the troubles of the world. We should not consider it to be little. It is much more useful than all the world you see around you. This idea will hold if we really love the truth. Loving the truth, even a little, will help us through the journey of this life.

☆

12 *Birth and Death*

Fear of death haunts the mind of even the bravest of people.

Everybody fears death, whether great or small, learned or ignorant; but there is no such thing as death. So-called 'death' is nothing but a natural corollary of the phenomenon of birth. The only way to avoid death is to avoid being born. It is not possible to be born and not to die.

Actually the individual Self, living in the body, is immortal. It gives up an old body in order to put on a new body, just as we give up our old clothes and put on new ones. If we are happy to discard an old garment and put on a new one, there is no reason to be unhappy when the Self discards an old body and adopts a new one.

An Indian went to Africa. When his money was finished there, he went to a money-lender to ask for a loan. Just then, there was a death in an Indian family living in that neighbourhood and the people of that family were weeping. The money-lender asked the Indian why his countrymen living in that house were weeping. He replied that it was a custom in his country to weep when there is a death in the family.

The money-lender asked again, 'And what do you do when there is a birth in the family?' The Indian said, 'Then we rejoice.'

The money-lender said, 'Then, if you are the sort of person who rejoices when receiving a thing but weeps when you have to return it, I certainly won't lend you any money.'

A person who dies has never written back to say what happened to him after death. Therefore, the only course open to us is to take authority from our holy scriptures on subjects relating to death and thereafter. We can find a lot of information there on these subjects. The following teachings from the Bhagavad-Gita tell us how to deal with death:

1. Forget the past. Do not fear the future either. Devote the present to the Param-Atman. A devotee of the Param-Atman never perishes.

2. For two half-hours a day, give up all duties and obligations; surrender yourself completely to the single care and protection of the Param-Atman. He will save you from all evil consequences, and therein would lie the end of all your worries.

3. One who sees Param-Atman in everybody and everything, and sees everybody and everything in Param-Atman—to him Param-Atman never becomes obscure and he never becomes obscure to Param-Atman.

We fear death because, under the influence of Maya, we have forgotten ourSelves. And it is this forgetting of the divine Self which makes for us all the troubles we get. It is not God who is the maker of our troubles.

☆

The one who is said to be born with a body at birth only discards the body at the time of so-called death. Death does not bring an end to the one who has the body. The one who takes and discards the body is a conscious being.

☆

Being part of the Absolute, the individual is fundamentally eternal, fundamentally all knowledge, fundamentally all joy. Surrendering oneself to God removes illusion. Then True Knowledge dawns and we realise there is no death for us, that no knowledge is hidden from us and that the fullest joy is always with us.

☆

13 Practice and Experience

In worldly life one needs money to build a house, to own a car, to buy food, clothes and other necessities. Without money one can't get these things. But there is a limit to what one can buy. One can buy a fountain pen, but one can't buy the ability to write. This, one has to acquire oneself. This experience cannot be bought. One may pay for the help of servants but the help given by family and friends is something different. It is given with feeling. This feeling cannot be paid for by anything. It can only be appreciated by the Self. Likewise in the spiritual world there are books to give you knowledge, but more knowledge doesn't make you a Realized Man. You need experience. Unless you go on the path, knowledge of the path is useless. What books can't give you, a teacher can. But above all, although you can get almost anything from others, realization you must experience yourself.

☆

Grace and effort do not work just single-handed. There is no such thing as grace without effort, nor can effort be fulfilled without grace coming into play. When sincere efforts are being made and there is no self-pride involved in the effort or achievements resulting from it, then spontaneously the grace starts flowing. With this

flow of grace the effort and its effects become
established, which immediately uplifts the effort of the
individual. If one just makes one's own effort and does
not create a situation where grace could come in, then
Rajas or Tamas usually take over and many other things
happen, and the individual has lost the line.

Alternatively, if one sat without making any effort
and did not bring oneself under discipline or the
activities concerned with the disciplines, and simply
waited for the grace to flow in, this would mean that
Tamas had completely taken over. You can be sure that,
in such circumstances, grace never appears to anyone.

Sattva is described mostly as light—a light which is
steady. So one of the major manifestations of the
presence of Sattva is this illumination of any type of
work one takes on. If one finds oneself afraid to tackle a
new situation or one has doubts on certain types of
subject, that instantly means lack of Sattva.

What can one do to change the situation so that there
is abundance of Sattva in one's being? The collection of
certain good qualities is essential. The good qualities are
these:

1. One should always love to speak the truth: so there is
no disparity between what one thinks and what one
says, or between what one says and what one does.
There should be complete correspondence of ideas with
activities.

2. Cultivate the love of people, encouraging them in

turn to express their love through certain types of activity.

3. Be magnanimous in dealing with those around you.

☆

If people have regularly come to hear the good words and yet have not found the point of rest, the main reason is the nature of their ingrained tendencies. They still have a certain disturbed element in them and it prevents them making their own all that is told to them and, when they go back, they again get engulfed in their previous tendencies. They should continue to meditate and reflect again and again about what they have heard so that in due course their previous tendencies will be removed and there will be room for taking in the new things they have been told.

To illustrate this:

There were two ants: one was living on a mountain of salt, the other was living on a mountain of sugar candy. It happened once that the two ants met and they talked about themselves. The ant who was living on the sugar candy was given a piece of salt by the other ant. When she tasted it, she said, 'It is horrible! How can they live on this?' The first ant invited the other to her home and so the second ant went to the sugar candy mountain with all her sisters and other ants. Thinking there wouldn't be enough for them to eat there, they all took a small piece of salt in their mouths. When they arrived, the sugar candy ant gave them a small piece of candy, but since they already had a small piece of salt in their mouths, the two tastes got mixed up—and they said, 'You praise your own home so much, but it is almost the same as ours'. Then the first ant said, 'Well, go and wash your mouths and then come again.' They did so and again tasted the candy and found that it was really sweet. So then they never went back to their own home.

The Truth is that one really is Atman and the Absolute, but one doesn't know this secret because of ignorance.

There was a dhobi (washerman). He used many donkeys to carry his load. One day he fell ill and asked his son to load the donkeys and take them with the washing. The son loaded them and tried to move them towards the river but they wouldn't budge an inch. Seeing they weren't tied up, he was surprised and went to ask his father. The father said, 'Oh, I should have told you about this! In the evening I touch their feet as if I am trying to bind them with a rope, and in the morning touch them again as if I have undone them'. The boy did the same, and then each donkey started to move. The donkeys felt they were not free; therefore they couldn't walk!

This is the condition of all human beings. The ignorance is illusion.

There are two types of people, those who work predominantly with head and those predominantly with heart. Those who work with head are usually prone to too much discussion, and those who work with heart accept the discipline or the discourse without any reasoning and like to get along with the work. But neither of them are really complete because the rational man, or the one who simply keeps on discussing and does not practise the discipline which is being given would not attain any level further, so he would not be able to reason in a better way and about subtler levels. The person who takes the discipline just on trust—if he faces a person with a different viewpoint, he might not be able to match up to him, and then he would have some inward doubt in his own heart about the discipline. Under the stress of the opposing ideas he might give up. Here is a story to illustrate this:

Two people were going to bathe in the Ganges and while they were walking the intellectual man said to the other, 'Look at this Creator—he must be a fool because he never knew what he was doing.' While they were going along they passed two types of plants—one was a pumpkin growing on the sandy soil above the river with many big pumpkins and six feet away was a mango tree. So the man with the head said, 'This is such a small plant and the Creator put such big fruits on it, and if you look at the mango tree, which is such a big tree it has such small fruits. So he must be a nut to have done such a thing'.

The other man, of the line of heart, couldn't reply and couldn't explain why he felt that the Absolute was not so foolish in doing this, so he kept quiet and felt sorry for himself.

When they were returning home from the bathe, they were tired and stopped for a little rest under a tree. They happened to sit under a mango tree, and while they were dozing one of the ripe mangoes fell on the nose of the man who was the intellectual. It hit him hard and he felt a lot of pain. At the same moment he exclaimed that now he understood why the Absolute made such small fruit on big trees. 'If he had done it my way, I would have been dead and gone!'

The moral is that both ways are insufficient. The real way is to bring these two together in unison. Then life is better and purposeful.

In India it is quite possible to get for a few pence a copy of the Bhagavad-Gita, which holds the philosophy of liberation but the essence and the truth and the knowledge which is enclosed in the Bhagavad-Gita cannot be bought even for a million rupees.

That truth or the knowledge of the Bhagavad-Gita is available only if one practises three-fold work. The three-fold work is as follows—the first is trust, faith. With faith one should prepare oneself and take to the work, in the service of the Absolute. The second is the sincerity with which one attends to the work or the knowledge which is being given, and one tries to understand and put the whole thing into practice again and again. The third is discipline to gain control over the senses and the mind. Control over the senses and the mind is essential, otherwise the disciplines are lost in due course.

☆

Dr. R. One is greatly helped if one's faith is pure and complete. I have perfect faith in the Shankaracharya, in my teacher, and the great men, but what I lack is faith in my discernment and my own nature. Above these is the Atman in whom I have faith, but this lack of faith in my nature hampers me all the time. If I get some access to self-confidence it's taken by the wrong thing, and I fall. I believe if one could somehow get more faith in the heart everything would be transformed.

H.H. This lack of faith is the last post of transformation. After having felled all other posts, when the aspirant comes to the last and can't cut it down, then he gets into a frenzy. He can't be blamed, for he acts only from deep habit. He even becomes angry with the helpers. He criticizes even the Absolute for being all-powerful and merciful. Why can't He help transform him?

The principle is that only by long practice can this last post be burnt by the fire of matured discipline. It does not go away by any outside force. Just as, if you pluck out weeds, they grow again until you take out all the roots hidden deep down in the ground, by long persistent practice of disciplined work the deep roots are burned slowly and when they are burned completely, then one can understand the uselessness of habit.

In the end it is up to the individual to decide once and for all that he is going to love only the truth and leave the rest. And he must stand by it. Only then is transformation possible.

☆

14 Systematic Steps

'Satsang' is good company. We get it through the company of holy books, through the company of holy men and through the company of Param-Atman. In order that we do not get confused and lost in a labyrinth of ideas, all these 'companions' are necessary; otherwise it is like treating yourself for a disease by reading medical books.

A frog sat beneath a lotus flower. Instead of enjoying its sweet fragrance, it only ate dirty worms from the mud below. A beetle knew what was good in a lotus; it sat over it and enjoyed the fragrance.

If we give some time to reading holy books, some time to thinking of Param-Atman, then our wisdom matures; darkness no longer frightens us, and we attain supreme happiness. Not only so, but we begin to radiate happiness which affects our surroundings as well as those around us.

If we do not practice Satsang in the above manner, then the thought of Param-Atman recedes to the background and ego comes in front. Ignorant worldly people, however, see no sense in all this and treat it as a waste of time.

One Shri Malviya used to meditate on Param-Atman for two hours daily. One of his friends said, 'Why do you sit idle for two hours each day? Instead of wasting them in this manner, you could do some work to benefit yourself or somebody else'. He replied: 'All right, maybe I am wasting two hours but you are wasting the other twenty-two hours as well!'

☆

There are seven successive stages like the steps of a ladder, each leading to the next, till the final stage is reached.
1. The first stage is good actions, which lead to—
2. The second stage, which is good thoughts.
3. Good thoughts lead to the third stage, which is decrease in bad thoughts.
4. Decrease in bad thoughts leads to the fourth stage, which is predominance of Sattva.
5. Sattva leads to the fifth stage, which is decrease in worldly attractions.
6. Decrease in worldly attractions leads to the sixth stage, which is giving up of worldly objectives.
7. Giving up of worldly objectives leads to the seventh and final stage, which is freedom from all thoughts about one's own self and one's personal profit.

☆

Q. What is the meaning of Sanatan?
H.H. The word Sanatan is made up of two words: Sada and Tan. Tan means the body, inner body. Sada means eternal, the 'Body of Eternal Religion', that is Sanatan Dharma. Sanatan Dharma is the religion of the Atman—the natural laws of the Atman. An example of a natural law is that, if somebody wants to speak lies all the day, he just can't do it. It is impossible because it is not the nature of the Atman to speak a lie. But if

somebody wants to speak the truth all day, he can do it. It is not impossible.

This is so because the nature of Atman is to be truthful—Atman is truth. The Sanatan Dharma is the original, the root of all religions, and of the religions which we see today.

It is not necessary at all to embrace Sanatan Dharma. Every religion contains it. 'If each one follows his own religion truthfully, he would for certain be following Sanatan Dharma. It is the basis of all religions and their centre. There is no need to change anybody's present religion.

The basic concept of Sanatan Dharma has been summed up in ten principles:

1. Having confidence and patience. If there is no confidence, there can't be patience. These two are united. So, Sanatan Dharma wants individuals to develop confidence and patience.

2. Having consideration and giving pardon and being tolerant of all the difficulties and awkwardness and faults of others, so that you provide them with space, and in due course, when they see there is no reaction, they may learn something better which you hold very dear to yourself.

3. The senses are very fast and if the mind is turbulent, receiving impressions from different sources, it is quite probable that sensual hunger and thirst may be inflamed because of the beautiful things being seen in the world, so every individual needs to have some control over the sensory appetite and its expression.

4. You should take only what you deserve, and consider everyone else equally deserving. So, do not take anything extra—all that you accumulate extra is

theft. You steal from the universe and you deprive other people. So do not keep anything more than what should be equally available to everybody else.

5. Cleanliness of body and mind. One has to learn to clean one's body, one's mind and one's heart, and for that one has to find a system through a teacher.

6. There is a natural course of use of the senses and these can be regulated; the rules are prescribed in every tradition, and from these one has to learn how to use one's senses within those limitations. One does not curb the use of the senses but regulates them. The curbing of excessive use will then take place naturally.

7. One is expected to use one's intellect or reason and find out the causes of things and use them as necessity may arise.

8. One has to acquire true knowledge, which is made manifest as far as Sanatan Dharma is concerned through the Vedas, which are supposed to be not man-made. Who made them nobody knows, so one has to acquire the knowledge of the scriptures.

9. The truth. There is only one truth about anything; there can't be two different truths about the same subject. Everybody in the world is hankering for truth, but it happens that people want their particular brand of truth, they are not eager or ready to accept that there can be something different. One may be right or wrong, and then rationalisation is necessary. Even thieves, robbers and evil men, they also wish that the people with whom they cooperate should speak the truth so that they do not get caught by the police! So truth is important not only for people in highly developed and cultured society; the need is everywhere; but somehow

people like to serve their own ends through their own concept of truth.

10. One should never get agitated under any circumstances. There may be occasions when a hard line is necessary, usually for the sake of education, but taking a hard line is not necessarily getting agitated. One can tell the difference between righteous agitation or wrong agitation. If one is wrongly agitated, one cannot take right action, so this has to be avoided.

Considering all these ten factors one can see that they do not only apply to the Hindus of India. They are for all human beings. That is how basic religion, or the concept of human religion, is Sanatan Dharma and the meaning of Sanatan is that the root of this concept, or idea, or religion has no end or beginning—it was not started by any particular man, and it will never end whatever happens. As long as human beings exist, these concepts will prevail. There is a Sanskrit verse which says that, if one learns to understand that one is part of this universe and one has equal status with everyone else, then give to others what you would like given to you. What pleases you should be made available for the pleasure of others—or do as you would be done by! This sums up the concept of Sanatan Dharma—it is a concept for humanity.

☆

15 Giving up

Whatever one sees in creation, all that lives and moves—one should use it fully and enjoy the Absolute in everything, but one should enjoy it with renunciation. One should not try to hold it or covet it. Just because the Absolute is always everywhere, one need not try to hold it; enjoy it—and give it up. 'Giving up' is the most simple philosophy which promises complete fulfilment of the individual's life, also liberation after having enjoyed it.

There is a story about Kach the son of Prajapati, the teacher of the Gods, the priest of the Gods. Kach, having gone through the proper education in the Vedic and Upanishadic texts, and having acquired all the knowledge that was available, came back to his father. His father asked him what he was intending to do. He said, 'The essence of all I have learnt is that renunciation is the best medium for life, so I would like to go the way of renunciation.' So he would not take up the activities of the priesthood, and he would not help in the household activities either; he just stayed in the house.

After some time, the father asked him whether he had really renounced everything. As far as the father could see, his son had renounced all work, but he still kept on moving, eating and using the amenities of the house. 'So what about that?' The son said, 'All right, I will renounce the house', so he left the house and went into the jungle and stayed there.

Later, the father visited him there and asked him what the situation was? The boy said, 'I can't say I have acquired complete peace, so it seems I have not yet renounced everything'. The father said, 'Yes, so it seems—your renunciation is not complete, otherwise peace would descend on you.' So he renounced the clothes he wore, the food he ate and all activity, yet he could not get real peace of mind.

'Now' he said, 'the only thing left to renounce is my body, so I must renounce my body', and he prepared a funeral pyre intending to jump into it. His father suddenly appeared and asked him to be sure that this would be the final renunciation. The son asked, 'But once I have given up the body, what else will remain to bind me to worldly things?'

The father replied: 'Your subtle body is not going to die with your physical body, and the activity of the subtle body (which has desires) will make it keep on wandering, and will not subside after the physical body is burnt. You will get another body when you are dead because there will be some desire in your subtle body, so burning the body is not the final answer—you are not going to get rid of this creation.'

So the son said, 'Well, if I cannot renounce, what else should I do?'

The father then said, 'At last you have asked me a question, so now it is possible for you to learn something! Give up all your learning and the final giving up—the final renunciation—will be the giving up of the very idea of renunciation. You are not giving up anything, everything is given up. By the idea of renunciation you are holding something in preference to other things—in fact, you are not renouncing; you are holding on very tightly to something less'.

The creation is such that everything has a purpose

and must fulfil its function; so it must keep circulating, it must be used. Use everything, and give up the idea that you are renouncing. Don't hold on to anything in this creation; that can only be done by this final renunciation of giving up the idea that you have anything. In fact, you have nothing. Everything is of the Absolute, everything is permeated by the Absolute; you use whatever you need, and the rest simply belongs to Him. This we must keep in our minds when we think of renunciation.

☆

Q. There are different sorts of desires—long desires, short desires, worldly desires and spiritual desires. Can these be made into one desire for consciousness?

H.H. The realm of desires and their fulfilment is the common realm. Some people have more desires than others; through all the disciplines we can learn to minimise our desires and as they become less, a greater force of consciousness would be available to us.

There is a way whereby there is no cessation of activity and yet there is no desire. There is no concept of achievement, there is no entanglement, no attachment to any activity, and yet there is a ready response to do whatever the moment demands of you. This surrender to the activity is a state where there is no hankering by the individual—whatever is needed he picks up and puts down instantly when it is time to stop. He thinks no more about it, and he can pick it up later if he is called upon to do the same thing again. This is unusual because in common life most of us like to complete the job, because completion of the work brings a sense of achievement—fulfilment of the desire.

Here is an example showing the two processes in action. When you go to the office to work you reach there, say, by nine o'clock and start work. At five o'clock you stop, pack up the papers and go home. On Saturdays and Sundays, when we are at home and not doing office work, we never look at our watches because we want to complete what we are doing. So without attending to time we continue the work and if we can, we finish it. If we can't, then next day we rise again with the same desire and we start again. There are big desires and there are small desires and there are routine desires like getting up early in the morning and performing certain acts necessary for our health, or for daily work.

Common man does not know that there is a way where there is no desire and yet the day is full of activity.

Judges seem to have this capacity. When they go into court, they have no preconceived ideas about the cases. A case is put before them; they listen to it with great attention and give their ruling or sentence as required. Having done so, they leave the court without taking worries about the case with them; and they can keep on doing this day after day without any involvement.

It is the involvement which we have to learn to give up—if our attachments are given up, then we can reach a state where we should be able to be active and do all our work without any loss of consciousness, without any loss of energy—no sense of achievement and no fulfilment of desire.

☆

The Mundaka Upanishad says: 'There are two birds, two dear friends, who have made their home on the self-same tree. The one pecks at the sweet fruit, while the other looks on in silence, not eating.

The first is the human spirit, who feels sad and bound by ignorance. But on beholding the power and glory of the universal, he becomes free from sorrow'.

They co-exist as they sit on the tree of creation and one of them enjoys the fruit of the tree. These two sweet friends are the Absolute and the individual. The individual is involved with the creation and its fruits. It feels as if it is seeing, eating, sensing and enjoying the world, and, in doing so, gets attached to the world, whereas the Absolute, although it is in and with the creation, is in no way involved with the creation and only watches and enjoys.

We do not see or understand that the changes take place in our nature and not in the Atman. Atman is not subject to change. One who understands this becomes very light and walks in freedom without carrying the load of the world. He is one who enjoys the drama in its true sense and never associates himself with the characters of the drama. Our job is simply to watch and enjoy.

☆

What we have to give up is the desire to derive benefit from our actions—and not the actions themselves. If we give up actions but continue to indulge in desires, then we would simply be pretending to give up. Before undertaking an action, an ordinary worldly man always tries to assess what benefit would accrue to him as a result. But a Realized Man undertakes it as a matter of duty, with no desire for its consequential benefits.

Before trying to do good to others, we should first try to improve our own selves. We cannot save a drowning man if we cannot swim ourselves.

Correct attitudes make real wealth. One who possesses this wealth is never poor.

☆

Some fifteen to twenty hundred thousand devotees had their dip in the holy waters of the Ganges and earned a profit. A trader is happy when there is a profit. But what about a loss?

In this 'trade' of life, all of us want a profit and want to avoid a loss. The first two verses of the Isa Upanishad tell us the way. They say:

1. The entire living and non-living world constituting this universe should be taken as covered by one single Param-Atman, as a manifestation of one single Param-Atman. Make your living in this world with the things thus provided to you, without desiring money from anyone else. But Param-Atman does not assert his ownership over what He gives to the world (like air, water, food etc.). Similarly, while using them for your living, you should not consider them to be belonging to you and yourself as the owner.

2. Desire a hundred-year-long life thus lived, and full of action. There is no other way to avoid a coating of evil while leading a human life.

People often complain that although they have been practising devotion or meditation over a number of years, yet they do not appear to be deriving any benefit from it. This is because their tendencies and nature have not changed.

We should bear in mind that, whatever the Creator has given to the world, He has 'given it up' to the world. He no longer asserts any ownership over it. We also should cultivate the habit of using and enjoying it as His gift and not as our own property. This attitude will correct our evil tendencies, and then the practice of devotion or meditation will begin to bear fruit.

It is not gold or worldly possessions that are evil; only 'identification' with them.

Once four men set out on a business trip, carrying fire-arms for protection. They met a Mahatma on the way. He warned them not to go that way as there was danger. They did not listen to him and said that they were well-equipped to face any danger. As they went further, they found a brick of gold lying on the ground. Rejoicing at their find, they wrapped it up in a piece of cloth with the idea of dividing it among themselves.

As night fell, two of them went to a neighbouring village to get some food and two stayed behind. When they had gone, those staying behind felt tempted to keep the brick themselves and conspired to shoot the other two when they returned.

Those who had gone to the village had a hearty meal. While returning with food for the other two, they also succumbed to the temptation of keeping the brick for themselves and conspired to do away with their companions. So they mixed poison with the food they were taking for them.

When they returned with the food, the other two shot them dead. But they were hungry. So they at once devoured the food brought for them. They fell asleep, never to wake again.

The next morning the same Mahatma passed there on his way to the river for his daily bath. He found the four lying dead and the brick of gold wrapped in cloth. He threw it into the river so that it could do no further mischief.

This is what happens in our daily life owing to our reasoning being polluted by evil tendencies. If we regard and use everything as a gift from the Param-Atman and thus practise devotion, then our reasoning becomes clear and we can lead the long and happy life as expressed in those verses in the Upanishad.

Evil associations cause evil tendencies in our reasoning, and they, in turn, result in evil actions. Good associations cause good tendencies and result in good actions. We should all try to achieve a life full of happiness and useful action by following this teaching of the Upanishad. Such a life would be a good worldly life, good for us and good for the world.

In one of the scriptures it says, 'This body is only flesh and bones; cease to be attached to it'. Transfer your attachment to the Atman. Because Atman is part of the Param-Atman, there is no difference between the two. Both are able to cut worldly bondages.

This body is the vehicle and Atman is the rider. Treat the rider separately from the vehicle. It is not easy to do so. It requires years of practice. We practise by thinking this body is God's property, not ours. This mind is God's property, not ours; everything is God's and nothing is ours. In this way we free ourselves from all attachments, all constraints. Again, this concept is difficult for those who think that 'I' is the physical body.

A Mahatma wished to live in complete solitude in order that he could meditate undisturbed at all times. He recounted his wish to a rich man. The rich man had an isolated rest house deep in the forest, rarely visited by mankind. He offered the rest-house to the Mahatma, and in addition provided a young servant to look after his comforts.

The young servant looked after him so well that his master's heart was moved. He asked the servant if he was content with his life, and if he could do anything to bring him happiness. The young man replied that he himself was content and happy, but he was afraid that his dead father had not achieved Self-realization as he was frequently appearing in his dreams. He asked the Mahatma for a remedy.

During the ensuing nights, the Mahatma was haunted by the problem of the young man's father. One evening the boy went to a neighbouring village to attend a marriage feast, telling the Mahatma that he would not return until the following morning. So the Mahatma locked up the house and went to bed. The young servant's bed was beside the Mahatma's and lay empty. The Mahatma's mind was filled with thoughts about the young man's father and his failure to achieve Self-realization. He was quite unable to sleep in peace.

The marriage feast was over by midnight, so the boy returned to the house immediately instead of waiting until the morning. When he got back, he climbed through the window and fell asleep on his own bed. At half-past three in the morning, the Mahatma awoke and saw the bed was occupied. In the darkness, he thought that the occupant must be the boy's father who had been haunting his son's dreams because he had not achieved Self-realization. He recited holy mantras and sprinkled blessed water over the body but the boy did not wake up as he was so deeply asleep. The Mahatma became frightened out of his wits. He opened the window and jumped out in order to get away. In his haste he fell over with a heavy thud. The noise awakened the young servant. He chased after the Mahatma with a heavy staff, thinking that he was a burglar. They recognized each other before many blows were sustained, and the mistake was cleared up.

In such a way, just a momentary thought, stealing unconsciously into the mind, will make its home there; then it appears later at some inopportune moment to cause mischief. Reels and reels of such thoughts are lying printed on our minds. They will not let us have peace, unless we develop the same attachment towards God as we now have towards the world.

Our desires are like so many strings that pull towards the world. Let this pull be towards God, instead of towards the world. The method is to establish the attitude that everything, including our physical body and mind, belongs to God. Whatever actions we do, including eating, drinking, reading, writing and looking after our duties, should all be dedicated to God.

The Bhagavad-Gita, ch.9, v.26, says: 'He who offers to me with devotion only a leaf or a flower, or a fruit, or even a little water, this I accept from that yearning soul, because with a pure heart it was offered with love.'

This is the meaning of devotion. Done in this way, your each and every action becomes an act of devotion and so becomes an act of worship to God, instead of being a worldly engagement. The worldly ties then are broken, and the presence of God supervenes.

In the absence of such a mode of thought, there is the world, and with the world comes all our trouble!

On the mast of a ship a bird was sitting quietly while the ship left the port and was going out to sea. The bird was confident that it could fly the distance back and reach its own place. After a long time with the ship far out to sea, it was evening, and the bird was thinking that its children would be crying for it at home, and it tried to fly home across the ocean. But it could not find the shore, so thought it must have mistaken the direction and returned to the mast for a rest. When it was rested it set off again in another direction, but the same thing happened—it could not find the shore because the distance was too great. It went to the South, to the North, to the East and West, but in the end it realized there was nothing it could do, so it returned to the mast and once more sat quietly.

Now it was confident again, but in another way—not that 'I can do', but 'I must go where the mast of the ship is taking me.'

So long as you are in the individual ego and not on the universal level, you will be thinking that you can do it yourself.

☆

Attachment means to consider as ours what really belongs to God. Our body, our house, our wealth, our son etc Give up this feeling and you get rid of all your troubles. Do not think that the world around you is insubstantial. Rather it is your feeling of attachment to it that is insubstantial. Whatever is happening around you is right. What is wrong about it is the view you are taking of it. If you could correct your viewpoint, you would be happy.*

Giving up can be done mentally and intellectually at all times and in all conditions. In this, there is no question of today or tomorrow, or of one or two days a week. Practise giving up all the time. You just consider the body, the mind and the intellect as belonging to the Param-Atman, and as offering all these to Param-Atman. This is what giving up means.

*See page 33

16 Singleness of Heart

You have asked for help in developing love or devotion to the Param-Atman, stating that your own capacity for love seems feeble. You should not worry on this account. Rather, you should remind yourself that the path of love is that very path on which Param-Atman is pouring all His favours and blessings all the time. Love and True Knowledge are two names for one and the same thing, which is a natural manifestation of the Atman and it comes to the surface spontaneously when the inner being is fully collected and attentive. Then you get the 'feel' of it.

Through your beneficial and holy efforts, let your own fullness see the fullness of the Param-Atman, and let the practice, the practitioner and the object of practice merge together to form one single identity. Then the world as such disappears and the Param-Atman appears in its place.

There is a Sanskrit poem which is the uttering of a man who seems to have offered everything to the Absolute. He says:

'Oh my Lord, my whole being is Yourself, and this mind which has been given to me is your consort.
The life-force, breath and energy which you have given me are your attendants.
My body is the temple in which I worship You.

Whatever I eat, or wear, or do is part of the worship
which I keep on performing at this temple.
Even when this body goes to sleep I feel I am in union
with You.
Whenever I walk, I feel I am going on pilgrimage to
You.
Whatever I speak is all in praise of You.
So, whatever I do in this world in any way is all aimed at
You.
In fact, there is no duality in this life of unity with
Yourself.'

This is the sort of situation which one has to find in
oneself, and this situation is charged with Sattva. Unity
is not something which one is aiming at, it is something
which one has to experience every moment in every
action, so that whatever one does is in praise or worship
of the Absolute. When that situation exists in one's
mind, one's being, then one is in constant union with
the Absolute.

There was a Mahatma living in a secluded place under a
tamarind tree. He did his devotional act of meditation
every day. There is a deity known as Narada and he is
supposed to be the messenger of the Absolute who
keeps on descending to earth gathering information to
keep the Absolute fully informed. He happened to be
making his rounds, and he came upon this Mahatma
and engaged him in conversation, wanting to know
what he was doing.
The Mahatma said, 'Well, this is all a drama, and at

the moment I am engaged in the drama of meditation, and who are you?' Narada replied that he was the messenger of the Absolute and came to collect information about all the devotees of God so that he could tell Him about their well-being. The Mahatma said this was excellent, as he could take a message, and Narada said, 'Yes, why not?' The Mahatma said, 'Ask Him when there will be a meeting'.

Narada went away, and came back after some time to the Mahatma, who asked him if there was any reply. Narada said there was a reply, but it was rather a bitter one and he would rather not give it as the Mahatma's heart would sink. The Mahatma said, 'But if there is any reply from the Absolute, my heart would never sink. Don't worry about it, just let me know the answer'.

Narada said, 'Look at this tamarind tree. It has very small leaves and millions of them; as many leaves as there are on this tree you will have to wait the same number of years, after which God will come to meet you; this is the message.'

At this the Mahatma burst into ecstasy, and started dancing with bliss, completely forgetting himself. Narada was quite baffled by this man, who, although told he had to wait millions of years before the union could take place, was dancing with joy. He asked, 'Wait—have you really understood what I have said?' The Mahatma replied. 'Yes, I heard,' and Narada said, 'What did you hear?' and the Mahatma said, 'As many leaves as there are on the tamarind tree, so many years will I have to wait and then He will come.' Narada asked 'Then why are you dancing?' The Mahatma said, 'I am not going to count the number of years and the leaves. All that matters is that I have had a message from the

Absolute, and He is going to meet me; He will never let me down. That is what really matters'. And once again he started dancing.

At that moment the Absolute Himself descended and embraced the Mahatma. Narada was very disturbed. He said, 'My Lord, I am your messenger, but don't let me be proved a liar. You said it would be so many years, and that is what I told the Mahatma, and you have broken your word and descended immediately! You didn't even wait an hour and you've fulfilled the promise which was supposed to wait years.'

Then the Absolute said, 'These things are for ordinary men; if there is somebody special, then questions of time and space and Gunas have to be ignored and the meeting must be instantaneous'.

The same applies to all these details about people of devotion or people of knowledge. If there is a rare case where there is nothing else, only devotion, nothing but a longing for truth, then the union could take place without delay.

☆

Q. When I came in here this morning, I felt complete reassurance of the absolute unity that exists in all things, and I was again completely certain that there is no need for any anxiety, and that all things are cared for. How can one hold that?

H.H. When one comes to certain places that have a special influence, there are two ways of holding this experience. One is by the mind. If it is held by the mind constantly and one reminds oneself about the experience and the taste of the experience, or the content of the experience, then in the course of time it becomes one's own.

The second way is to hold by faith—and that is held in the emotional body of the individual. It holds it very tight; this is where it is held totally. Having held this from these two standpoints, from faith and from mind or thought, then it becomes one's own. Then wherever, or under whatever circumstances, or under whatever influences one may be living, one will never lose this experience which has become one's own. And over and above that, one would be able to transmit these influences wherever one goes, provided this influence is held by mind and by the emotion through faith.

A father does everything he can for his child, and when he takes the child on to his lap to feed it, the child may take a little of the food and try to put it into his father's mouth. Now, that tiny piece of food which the child puts into the father's mouth pleases him so much, that all the troubles brought on by the child are forgotten.

The Absolute, or the Atman, wants the human heart in its simplicity and directness. When that has been dedicated, everything will follow in the course of time, and one need not worry whether man's actions are small or big, good or bad, efficient or inefficient. That doesn't matter—the real dedication He requires is only of the heart.

☆

The Atman never questions because He has no reason to question, so whenever a question arises, it never arises from the Atman. It always arises from the individual ego which is not fully realized. It is not the Atman, it is not the Absolute, so it wants to know, and it is necessary that there should be questions because full realization has not taken place. As long as full realization has not taken place, the questions must arise. But if one allows the ego to answer the questions, then one will be in trouble.

Should one put the questions to the Atman? That is a possibility. If the Atman has no questions, certainly He must know everything; He must also know the question in the individual's mind, so should one question the Atman who knows the question already?

One cannot question the Atman—one cannot ask questions of the Atman. But one can pray to Him. Be humble, and put up a prayer to the Atman to resolve the question—that is a way to appeal to the Atman, and then the proper answer will be available.

In love you always give and don't demand in return. By giving, you allow things to happen.

When people love someone, they forget that real love means no demands from the beloved.

In dedicating to the Absolute or to the Self, the most important part is the heart, and that is very simple. If that is properly achieved in its simplicity, all the rest should not bother one, because nothing else is very important. One can see from many examples that this is so. Here is one:

There was a great elephant who was proud of his size and strength, but when he went for a bathe he was caught by a crocodile in mid-stream and dragged out of his depth into the deep water. He was helpless and couldn't do anything; but just when he was about to be drowned he happened to catch with his trunk a lotus flower floating on the river, and offering that flower to the Absolute, to his God, he begged Him to save his life. So pure was his offering that God came running barefoot from his throne.

One might wonder how one could dislodge the Absolute and cause him to come barefoot from His throne by just a little flower! But it was not the flower, it was the spirit behind the flower—it was the heart which prayed.

☆

True love has no motive. It is all-forgiving to the beloved; the whole life becomes a service so that the beloved may be pleased; it is for his pleasure that everything is done, without demanding anything at all. If there is any difficulty of time and space or meeting between the two, true love does not diminish or lessen. It rather increases. The other love, which also works through emotion, is used only for the achievement of certain results; if the result is not forthcoming, then this love turns into bitterness and anger. Thus one can see, that if love turns negative, it is impure love. If no tension arises and devotion is always flowing, then one can say it is pure love.

☆

A good man who wants to go on the spiritual path speaks what he feels, and does what he speaks. That is, he speaks from pure feeling. When he has impure feelings, he tries not to speak or rush into action or express them. A bad man does the reverse: he feels something and says something else; he says something but does something else.

If one really speaks what one feels and does exactly what one says, then this builds up a man's inner strength and, because of the clarity and unity of his mind and sincerity of his heart, the way becomes fairly clear for him.

This is the sort of purity one gets only if one follows pure feelings and expresses them in true words, and does exactly as one says. If one keeps this consistency, then one would grow—one would become more serious and have more strength of character. This brings unity into a man and creates a sort of depth, and to this unity and depth of the individual the glory of the Absolute descends.

Q. When, for a while, ego is quiet and one's role is being naturally fulfilled, love seems to be the unifying force, and discriminating mind seems to work within it—is this the right relationship?

Q. How may the heart be opened?

H.H. In response to the second question about 'opening the heart', when one brings to one's knowledge the different aspects of the glory of the Absolute, then one feels grateful for the bounty which is being provided for the individual, and immediately the hard heart melts. If one feels, however, how little one is, compared with the glory of the Absolute which is being manifested all around, then that will open the heart. So, being grateful alone is the key to opening the heart.

As for the first question, this is exactly what is meant by the 'unity of thought and word and deed, when you think and say what you feel, and do what you say'. This, again, is very much connected with the opening of the heart itself. One penetrates into the stream of bliss, through which everything can be properly and nicely regulated, and one ceases to feel any difficulty in one's activities or one's relationship with people.

☆

Love and knowledge are the same thing but the function of love is to join together and that of knowledge to tell, to illuminate.

In love, knowledge is helpful. For strengthening knowledge, love is essential. In the absence of love, knowledge would not be powerful enough to influence people. Knowledge only helps us to decide what is right and wrong, but it cannot alter things; love can alter them.

Without love, knowledge is incomplete and without knowledge love is incomplete because, in the absence of knowledge, love would go away. If there is knowledge, then love would be maintained. As love increases, knowledge also goes on increasing. Without knowledge, love is not expansive; and without love, knowledge is not allowed to play its full part.

☆

Q. When through grace one comprehends a big idea, what can one do to preserve it?

H.H. Whenever one gets something valuable in the physical world, one likes to keep it in a safe place, in such a place that one can easily make use of it, or look at it and get some pleasure from it. One sometimes puts such things into safes and, when the need arises, one takes them out and uses them.

In the same way when we get some big or good idea from the grace of the Absolute, from the grace of a Realized Man, from the scriptures, or from good company, the best thing to do to preserve it, is to keep it in a safe place. The safest place is the heart itself. That is where one can keep it and then make use of it later. Only the wise can keep it in their heart because the fool assembles all the rubbish that he collects and keeps that in his heart. So when he gets a really valuable thing he has no room left to keep it in his heart, thus he cannot hold it nor make any further use of it. What really matters when one gets a gift of grace is love, and the importance which one gives to it. This will decide what one does with it. If one loves something, one will not forget it. This is natural. If one attaches importance to something it will not be lost from the phenomenal mind and thus it can be used and preserved.

Q. What exactly is meant by keeping it in the heart?

H.H. Anything which we remember again and again and seek for—that must be in the heart. This is how one can check if something has been placed in the heart or not. As to how to attach importance to it so that it may reside in the heart and be remembered again and again, this can only be done by good company. There are three types of good company—company of the Self, the company of the Realized Man and the company of colleagues or companions. It is only through continuous effort with good company that an attitude of importance can be established towards a certain idea. If one gets that by grace, one could preserve the idea.

☆

Even better than praying is holding the thought of Param-Atman in the mind. We can only pray for a short time, but we can keep this thought in the mind all the time. Param-Atman is very generous. A little thought of Him melts His heart.

Just as a son has some elements of his father, similarly all of us carry some element of Param-Atman. But merely knowing this is not sufficient.

For example, we all know that wood is inflammable. This knowledge by itself would not create a flame. When we rub two pieces of wood vigorously together, a flame appears from the wood itself without application of any external fire. Similarly, the flame of knowledge springs up from the rubbing together of our thoughts, and it burns away all that is undesirable.

To know is merely knowledge, but to acknowledge is to love. Yet even to know and to acknowledge are not enough; we should also think. Devoting the mind to Param-Atman and remembering Param-Atman should be a constant practice. Then life would flow naturally and doubts would dissolve by themselves.

☆

When the idea that Atman alone is truth and the rest is Maya or illusion has been fully appreciated, then one will experience expansion of light, power, knowledge and service, and accordingly the limited ideas of individuality and relationships will break their barriers and go on extending in proportion to the depth at which this idea is rooted in the being. The being will be full of enthusiasm and one will be naturally able to know more, teach more and be of service to many more people than before. The world would become a family. The limited would become unlimited, small would become large, and darkness be transformed into light. Love would prevail everywhere. The individual would love all and all others would love the individual.

In the alchemy of the heart everything is taken care of, and the process shapes itself as the devotee wants it to shape. Faith is the most important thing—faith in the unchanging Absolute, and faith in the meditation. One simply steadfastly keeps on going and in the course of time it will become natural and give the needed truth.

If once during our lifetime an unshakeable faith in Param-Atman is established, that is, that we belong to the Param-Atman and Param-Atman belongs to us, then we are out of reach of all harm. At that stage things change their properties for us; a harmful drug becomes harmless. This is how a cup of deadly poison given to Mira, a perfect devotee, lost all its poisonous properties in her hands. We know that substances change their properties during a chemical reaction. Why, then, can this not happen on a more subtle level where much more powerful forces come into play? Faith can change all that. It cleanses you, purifies you, decorates you, and presents you before the Param-Atman at your best.

The Param-Atman alone is unchanging; it always remains the same. But Param-Atman is also manifesting through all the different forms which we encounter and through which we derive knowledge. It is quite possible, therefore, that our concept of Param-Atman would keep changing. One may wonder since one's concept is changing, what really is happening. In fact, there is nothing wrong in all this; one's concept must keep on evolving, and one's knowledge and concept of Param-Atman will continue to become subtler and subtler. However, within this ever-changing concept of the unchanging Absolute, there is one thing which never needs to be changed and that is faith in the Param-Atman. If one has faith—complete unchanging faith—then one should not worry about changing concepts.

17 Giving back

The basic meaning of initiation is to connect the individual with the universal (Param-Atman). The mantra given enables one to establish a connection with the Lord. After initiation, whatever one eats, one should think of it as a gift. After initiation, whatever we do, we do it with surrender to the Almighty; whatever we receive for our own use we should regard it as 'Prasad'—a gift from the Almighty. We must carry the idea that we own nothing. Everything has now become God's; we are using everything with His permission, and not as owners. This helps with the elimination of the individual ego—then the pure realization of the Self develops.

Whatever we have is part and parcel of the cosmos. This body represents the earth of the cosmos; mind represents moon, the power of seeing represents the sun, etc. So that whatever we have, the individual is a particle of the cosmos. Normally 'Prasad' is associated with what we offer to the Lord and then receive back. It is the gift from the Lord but, before we get the gift, we make our offering. The best way, connected with devotion, is to regard whatever we have as a present from the Lord. In whatever circumstances we have been placed—that is also the Prasad of the Lord.

For instance—we cook our food; then, if we offer it first to the Lord and take it as a gift, that will be very healthy. It will be very helpful for spiritual progress if we accept everything only after first offering it. It is so even in doing our work, performing our duties. Supposing we are in the profession of law—when we start our day's work we first offer it to Him, 'With your help, God, with your Prasad I'm going to argue this case.'

So, whatever we do, we should first offer it and make it a Prasad. This purifies your mind and your body, and you become more suitable—eligible for God's spiritual roles.

Dedication to the service of the Param-Atman and to other people in thoughts and actions, at all times and in all circumstances, is the way to stabilise your mind in your own great Self.

No action by itself is high or low, good or bad. It is the motive behind it that elevates or lowers it. Even the lifting of baskets can be great for peace of mind, whereas even Samadhi accompanied by attachment would not give any.

Q. How do we practise devotion?

H.H. You don't have to prepare a very long scheme for practising devotion. Whatever you are doing, you can continue to do the same thing; you have only to change your approach. If you are doing anything with a view to some personal gain, then the approach should be: 'I am doing this not for any gain, but as a service to God. What I am eating, I am not eating just for my own satisfaction, but as an offering—it has been given to me by the Lord to enable me to serve Him. So that whatever you do, you connect it with the Lord—that will become devotion—you don't have to change your course of action; the action will be the same, but the object will be different.

1. Physically, be everybody's servant—devote yourself to universal service.
2. Emotionally, give importance to the Supreme Being, always remembering His never-ceasing good will and benevolence.
3. Intellectually, identify yourself as One with Param-Atman who witnesses everything impartially and reveals Himself in all that you perceive.

A Mahatma was approached by an ordinary man and asked what he should do. He did not feel he could undergo much discipline, so what was the simplest form? The Mahatma said he could find Param-Atman if he just kept running and when he fell exhausted he would find Param-Atman.

The man asked, 'If Param-Atman could be found by running, why not just by sitting?' 'Yes', the Mahatma replied, 'perhaps by sitting but the question is, what are you sitting for? If you are sitting for the Param-Atman, Param-Atman will meet you. If you are running for the

Param-Atman, Param-Atman will meet you there. You can do anything, it does not really matter. The real crux is whether you are doing it for the sake of Param-Atman, or for something of this world'. The Mahatma continued by saying that the unity is already there, nobody has to acquire it, but because we have all forgotten our unity, we are only required to give up our ignorance, give up our forgetfulness by any means.

If you try to do anything, however gloriously you may do it, just to fulfil your worldly commitments, you will find that the union which is already there will not be experienced. So the thing to decide is that one is doing everything—even digging the earth or anything else one likes to do—for the Param-Atman.

There is something in all of us, which is special or outstanding. Some are intelligent, some are unintelligent, some are strong, and some are weak; some are learned and some are ignorant; some are rich and some are poor.

Each should try to please God (or serve God, or worship God as the case may be) with that attribute in which he chiefly excels. This is the path of least resistance. It is sure to work, as it has always done in the past.

The method is, do what each of you is meant for, and do it in a spirit of service to God. Let eating, drinking, sleeping, bathing etc., all be dedicated to God. This is the correct worship, and the correct devotion.

A strong and deep affection lives in our heart for our child, or father or wife; yet we go about our normal business and do not recite their names all the time. This is exactly how we should keep God in our heart and go on doing our duties at the same time.

Do your normal duty in service to God and worship of God. You can reach God through it. But if you do not like your own duties and take up other people's duties because they appeal to you more, you will lose your way and ruin yourself. Thus, doing your own duty and dedicating it to God is the golden rule to peace and happiness.

When you have some sort of love, the effect is that you bring enthusiasm into the work to keep it continuous. To bring about this situation, if we think and try to impress upon ourselves that all the work which we are undertaking for any result is only in the service of the Absolute, so that we offer as our service whatever we do, then the individualistic approach or the egoistic approach would not intervene in the work.

That is the true way and one should see that one serves the Absolute, and does not think to achieve things personally by one's own deeds.

We would greatly benefit if we offered all our actions to Param-Atman.

There was a boy who had lost both his parents. He was very poor and wanted to join a school to study. To do this he needed money for school fees and stationery but he had no money to buy them. All this caused him considerable worry. By chance he met a Mahatma and told him his difficulties. The Mahatma gave him some advice. He told him to write a letter to Param-Atman. 'Write the letter like this: Oh, my father, the absolute Param-Atman, please help me. I am very poor, my parents are dead, I have no money to pay my school fees, buy books or continue my studies.' 'How shall I post it?' he asked. 'Address it to the Param-Atman', the Mahatma told him. He did as he was told, writing the letter, and addressing it simply to Param-Atman. He then put it in the letter box. The box was cleared and the letters taken to the postmen who sorted them out. One asked, 'Where does Param-Atman live?' They showed the letter to the postmaster who asked them to bring the boy to him. The boy was brought to the postmaster, who adopted him and looked after all his expenses. The boy had the highest education and eventually became a judge.

(The judge himself told this story to His Holiness.)

In the same way, if we offer all our actions to Param-Atman, dedicate all our action to the Param-Atman, then Param-Atman fulfils all our necessities and those of the people who are connected with us. Offering all our actions to Param-Atman doesn't mean that, after earning some wages, we lose them by offering them to Param-Atman. It is just that mentally we offer our wages to Param-Atman. The money is ours but, when we use it, we can regard it as a gift from Him. We should adopt that attitude. Having learned that, we should treat it as belonging to Param-Atman, then we use it as a gift, not as our own.

☆

The meditation is a discipline designed to produce Sattva and the stability which comes with Sattva. Once you have got some Sattva out of meditation, you have to use it. You have to choose the way you wish to use it either by loving people, or by helping people or doing some other activity pleasing to God. You will see that whatever you do, you will do it with more efficiency and goodness. The activity of meditation is not for the sake of meditation itself, otherwise it will become void. It produces Sattva, and Sattva has to be used for the type of activity which one chooses to take on in the worship of God or any other activity for the spiritual advancement of the individual.

In the realm of the Atman there are no barriers of space or time; we are all united, and there is no separation of any sort. The Absolute desires that goodwill and goodness prevail everywhere, irrespective of land or time.

Index